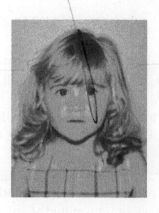

ANNIE RAINEY

Daisy Can't Talk © Annie Rainey 2020

Published by
Candy Jar Books, Mackintosh House
136 Newport Road, Cardiff, CF24 1DJ
www.candyjarbooks.co.uk

ISBN: 978-1-913637-13-2

Edited by Keren Williams
Editorial: Shaun Russell

Printed and bound in the UK by
Severn, Bristol Road, Gloucester, GL2 5EU

Nick, thank you for being our grumpy mad Irishman, for staying with us, providing everything we have ever needed and ignoring (and laughing at, so annoying) all my screaming banshee outbursts. I would never tell you to your face, and doubt you will read this, but if you happen to glance at this page I just need you to know that without you as my husband I doubt there would ever have been a happy ending. You have made all our lives amazing by being the calming voice of reason (can't believe I have just written that), yes you piss me off, yes you can be exasperating, but you are a fabulous husband and father and the kindest human I have ever known. I love you.

Harvey, you are the funniest, most caring, loving older brother a girl could ever want for. Daisy's eyes light up for you, you have that special bond with her, you are her hero I'm sure of that. I am confident that should anything ever happen to me or your dad, you will be there for Roo, that is such a comfort and I know that in you, I (we) at least got something right. Thank you for just being the perfect son, for just being you, a bloody fantastic specimen of fabulousness. You're my world.

Daisy, what can I say. You will never know what you have added to my life. I believe you've made me a nice person (lots would disagree). You have by default introduced me to a world I didn't know existed, but that world is one that needs a voice. You have made me laugh, cry (too much) and have given me an empathy that we all should share. I would offer you my life if I knew it could be switched as I'm so sorry your's isn't how it should be. I truly hope you are happy in your little world. I just hope we have, so far, given you the best years that we could. I am deeply sorry you couldn't be fixed. Always be you, our fearless, feisty, little Roo x

Introduction

I had it all, a successful, hard-working husband who would give me anything I wanted (within reason), an adorable handsome young son, beautiful house, cars, handbags, jewellery – you name it, I had it. Now, I was pregnant and expecting a girl. Life couldn't get any better.

We hadn't planned Daisy. I guess she was just meant to be. In fact she's lucky to be here at all. You see, my husband Nick didn't want another child and to say he wasn't very happy the day I broke the news to him is a big understatement. Very early on in the pregnancy, I was offered the choice by my fabulous husband to rid ourselves of her.

'It's our marriage or that bunch of cells,' I was told.

Well, I chose 'that bunch of cells'. We are still married. The rest is parked in history. We never really spoke much. I juggled work, childcare, housework and Nick, well, he juggled the gym, swimming, golf and work. He did reluctantly accompany me out of duty to the odd scan, but then he would rush back to work and nothing was said, not interested.

Nick is your typical man's man. He didn't like to discuss anything that involved babies and removed himself

2

from my pregnancy. It was lonely. Harvey, my son, was hard work. He was a very clingy child and even though I read all the books ever published on 'how to be mother earth' it just never seemed to come naturally to me. I did my best and Harvey grew into a happy, confident little boy, but none of it was thanks to Miriam Stoppard's books explaining how to be the perfect mum, of which I read many. No, I learned by default as I struggled through the early years.

When Harvey was three and a half, Daisy was born by elective caesarean (that's another story). She was absolutely beautiful – big and beautiful. Nick didn't gush at her arrival apart from the sarky quip, 'she looks like a right bruiser'.

He did attend the birth though, but wasn't really there, if you know what I mean? I could tell he felt uncomfortable with the whole scenario. In fact, the following day he only popped in to see mother and child so that he could park in the hospital car park and go to see Arsenal in the FA cup final. They lost, so upon his return he wasn't the best company.

Daisy was like my own living doll. I had bought so many pretty dresses and I changed her even if she looked at me sideways. I loved dressing her in cute little outfits, she always looked spotless, flawless and dreamy. I was so lucky. For the first few weeks at home she appeared to be a really good baby. Perfect, in fact. I felt more confident with her than I did when I had Harvey. Too confident probably, as on one occasion, I chopped the skin off the top of her finger whilst attempting to cut her nails. 'Shit'. Boy did I panic, there was a lot of blood, a lot, but all was well.

Nothing a mother's suck couldn't cure.

She was a very hungry baby feeding every two hours, it was exhausting, but she would then sleep for one maybe two hours so that I could recharge and refill the mammary glands.

This is going to be great, I thought, *a natural feeder, good sleeper and a beaut.*

Then things started to change.

Chapter One

14 days to 15 Months

Daisy didn't stop crying! I tried everything and, believe me, nothing worked. The many doctors we graced didn't care, insisted she had colic, but she cried in every waking moment of every waking day.

For weeks leading into months, I purchased and researched every treatment available for colic, even resorting to some looney tune 'cranial osteopath', who soothed her head in his spindly hands until she was somewhat hypnotized, insisting he'd fixed her 'alignment'.

Gosh, had this worked? Had it hell. Five minutes into the journey home, and fifty pounds poorer, she was back to her oh so familiar screeching.

No one ever visited me and Daisy. Well, if they did, they only ever stayed for a sip of coffee then the ridiculous excuses would emerge: 'Sorry, have to go and take the cat to the vet' and 'Must go, not long until the school run' (the time only being eleven o'clock!)

I became incredibly envious of anyone who had a quiet baby. What was I doing wrong? What was wrong with her? Why did she hate me so much? I began to think I had borne the spawn of Beelzebub!

Friends I had spent many a happy evening drinking and socializing with when Harvey was a baby were now fizzling out on an almost daily basis. No one wanted to share a room with Daisy, not even me.

Nick was never a nine-to-five type of person at the best of times, however, now we were lucky if he was working six-to-eight. He just didn't want to hear her bellowing and I couldn't blame him. Life was becoming increasingly difficult, torturous in fact.

Months passed and I had to get help. The health visitors weren't much use. Daisy was reaching all her milestones, but kept failing her hearing test. We were referred to the hospital for tests, but they were inconclusive. Could she be deaf? Not possible. She woke if I dared to creep out of the bedroom at night!

After endless tests and months of antibiotics for glue ear, it turned out, to our great relief, that Daisy wasn't deaf. But, if she wasn't deaf what on earth was wrong with her? Why did she cry so much?

I would do anything I could not to listen to her cries. I would put her in the garden in her buggy and sit in the kitchen just watching her cry from the window, crying myself, sobbing for hours. Heaven knows what the neighbours must have thought, but thinking about it, if they were concerned they never offered to help.

I was in a completely hellish script. A script that so far had no happy ending, one that I could see no escape from. I would drive for hours and hours with the music on, the radio cranked up just so I could escape. She seemed much more content in the car, but as soon as I returned home, the pain of hearing her cries would re-ignite and it was back to square one.

That year of my life turned out to be one of utter sadness all round, for not only did I have the sadness of not being able to comfort my beautiful baby, but I also lost my father to cancer just after Daisy turned one.

His death was so sudden and a massive shock. I felt huge guilt, still do, that I wasn't a great daughter. Always selfish, always right, never wrong, no love to give. He was a very calming man and made me feel adequate as a mother whenever I visited. He called Daisy 'Dozy' which were probably wise words in hindsight.

His words were always careful and I found him comforting. He had a dry sense of humour which I loved, but he could also be cutting, which I loved! Now he was gone, my heart was aching, a daughter who never expressed any love to her parents – maybe because it was never really offered – was breaking. I had lost an important rock. I would never see him again. I needed him and now he was gone. I still see the sadness in his eyes when I close mine, an image that is with me now.

My life felt like it was spiralling out of control. This wasn't the plan. What had happened to my perfect world, where had it gone?

Chapter Two
15 Months

Over the summer months following her first birthday, Daisy seemed to calm down slightly. Either that, or I had just become immune to her cries and moans. Whatever it was, I felt more in control.

By the age of fifteen months, Daisy was starting to show definite signs of improvement. She now had a few words, Mum, Dad, Daisy, Harbey, car, dolly, the usual.

The crying and moaning was more of a rarity and she was finally more content in her own company. Both myself and Nick thought she was a bit of a fast learner, as she seemed to reach certain milestones so much earlier than Harvey had. Lazy Harvey didn't say a word until he was two years five months and that word was dipsy, bloody dipsy!

Daisy was cruising at speed around the furniture and used a baby walker with such ease. Crashing into everything, she was a weapon on wheels. She would sit happily in her highchair and bang and thrash her toys ferociously, as you would expect. At last, she was turning a corner, the cries were easing, her personality, albeit a bit boisterous, was peeking out. We, as a family, were slowly starting to enjoy this beautiful, and I mean beautiful, little girl. We had jumped a huge hurdle, so we thought.

Chapter Three
16 Months

The brief period of almost normality sadly didn't last long. Daisy started to fall into a silent world. Within a few weeks of receiving her MMR jab, Daisy had taken a backward step. We felt she must have had an underlying illness, but no doctor listened. She was a good weight and rosy cheeked, but something wasn't right, *she* wasn't right. I had been to the surgery so many times in her short life I must have been on some sort of 'Munchausen by Proxy list', and if I wasn't I should have been.

Daisy was back to suffering from lots of ear infections and was constantly on antibiotics, so I guess we thought that her sudden lack of interest in playing, babbling, etc., was due to this upset in her life. She would soon 'recover', we just had to be patient.

She started to lose interest in cruising around the furniture and would be quite happy to just sit, whine (you know, that unbearable type of whine) and generally be a pain in the arse. Nothing interested her. She just existed really, but needed my constant attention to keep her calm. She didn't sleep well and, because we slept together, I didn't sleep well. Frankly, I didn't like her.

It was around this time that we became concerned about

her 'head banging'. She would throw her head to the ground and seem to feel no pain. Again, doctors told me it was just a phase, they weren't interested. Her forehead was always purple, no one ever questioned the bruises. My walls and floor were her toys, the harder the surface the better the thrill. Corners of walls were particular favourites, she got a better reaction from my screams and her pain. It was an awful time for us.

I decided I had to try to get on with life and do the things all the other mums did. I mistakenly chose to take her to one of those awfully pretentious mother and toddler groups, but this just drove me insane.

I couldn't sit amongst those pathetic women who knew it all. 'Oh, Emily doesn't stop chattering', I would hear in one ear and 'Jake is such a joy to have', would hit me in the other. I hated it. I hated everyone.

All those women ever talked about were their precious Einstein's and all I wanted to do was escape even thinking about Daisy for an hour or so. I wanted to forget I had her and chat about celebrities, handbags, fashion, anything except bloody kids. I stopped meeting up and was soon living a very solitary life during daylight hours, just me and 'the child from hell'.

However, things changed at her eighteen month checkup. A health visitor showed real concern. I didn't appreciate at the time the enormity of her concerns, I was just thankful I wasn't going mad and that someone could see something wasn't quite right too.

The health visitor arranged for Daisy to be referred for a developmental assessment. Something called a 'Ruth Griffiths

Test'. *Bizarre name*, I thought.

'Nothing to worry about,' she said and smiled.

But I knew, I knew problems would be unearthed. Call it mother's instinct.

That health visitor sitting in my living room on that rainy, miserable day was the beginning of a massive turning point in our lives. One that would alter everything and turn our world upside down.

Chapter Four
18 Months

I'll never forget the day I had to take Daisy to her first meeting with a specialist. I arrived flustered, after struggling to find the place amongst the one-way systems and maze of terraced houses. However, we arrived, Daisy looking beautiful and angelic amidst a run-down, grubby, dusty community-type centre. Sitting outside the room were a few other families with apparently 'normal' looking children, albeit unruly.

We waited our turn and then entered the room. All I can say is that it wasn't exactly Daisy friendly. Standing in the corner of the room was a precariously placed skeleton. Alongside it was a height measuring contraption and dotted around the room were several boxes and files, and numerous tables all of different sizes. It was as if we were sitting inside a store cupboard, ewww!

Sitting at a table was a women, who would best be described as urgently needing a hairdresser and stylist. Daisy and I entered the room. I immediately warned 'Scarecrow Woman', or Worzel for short, that Daisy could possibly cause a bit of damage, especially to the size zero pile of bones in the corner of the room. She just smiled and assured me no child had ever been able to knock over her roommate.

It was as if Daisy could understand, for no sooner had the words left her lips, than Worzel's friend had been dislocated from every angle.

Ouch, I thought, as I peeled Daisy's grasp from a thigh bone still semi-attached to said skeleton. Daisy was frantically trying to put the bone in her mouth, blimey, how shameful.

Taking the bone and its protruding screws from her mouth and wiping away the dribble mixed with Quavers, I carefully placed it on the now 'pile' on the floor.

'Sorry. Sorry.' The words echoed from my mouth. You'll find I use those words a lot.

Worzel said nothing, just jotted down notes on a dog-eared pad. I picked Daisy up and secured her in her buggy, safe in the knowledge that no harm could now come to the store cupboard. Ahh, if only we were born with hindsight! The chaos over, Worzel opened up a brown 'budget day' looking briefcase. Inside were numerous little objects ranging from toy horses to a comb and mirror set.

I was intrigued. What could be next? It was quite exciting. The objects were placed on the table opposite our seat, excitedly Worzel started combing, yes, combing, the horses mane, while clip-clopping noises and attempts at neighing poured from her lips.

I looked to see if there were any cameras in the room. Surely this couldn't be for real, this woman couldn't be for real? She was a fruit loop, away with the fairies. Worzel then handed the comb to Daisy.

'Daisy comb horsey's hair,' she gushed, looking eagerly at a now bored Daisy, whose fingers were lodged up her own nose, as she passed her the comb and horse. With a flash of light, the horse entered Daisy's mouth quickly followed by the comb and then by several other objects from the chancellor's case.

A flushed Worzel pleaded with Daisy to release her objects; they were after all specifically chosen for this test. I bribed Daisy with a Quaver that I had found on the step of her buggy. All artifacts unceremoniously left my little angels mouth, landing on Worzel's jotter with a rather soggy and sticky residue. Quavers are never a good look when soggy but they have saved my life many, many times.

Wiping her precious specimens, Worzel carried on un-perplexed, revealing a doll and a toy slide from her case.

'Wheeee,' she shrieked, as she pushed the doll down the slide. 'Daisy do it.' Handing Daisy the doll and slide, I watched in a knowing way as Daisy put the doll in her mouth and removed the head. I must admit I did panic a bit, because the head was gobstopper size, but Daisy has an amazing gag reflex. Out came dolly all slimy and stunned.

Worzel scribbled frantically, assuring me that everything was fine. My guard down, while I was dreaming of being whisked from the room by Brad Pitt, Daisy wriggled her way out of the buggy, CRASH! Down came the height contraption and boy did it crash. How could Daisy cause so much havoc in such a small space of time? Worzel was lucky to escape with her life, as she was so nearly speared by the antique medical museum piece. Funnily enough, our very first meeting with a specialist had come to an abrupt end and both Daisy and I left the store cupboard to await the report.

Weeks passed, then we seemed to be inundated with appointments to see more specialists. For the second appointment, Daisy and I were accompanied by Nick.

Jeez, this must be serious, I thought. He'd never really shown any interest in Daisy before this date.

We waited in the grim waiting room full of children of all sorts of disabilities. My heart bled for some of them. I felt a bit of a fraud sat there with Daisy the Destroyer, as I didn't think she was disabled in any way. She was just different, just Daisy.

You know the way it is, you sit there for what seems an eternity, quietly trying to appease your child wondering who will next be called by the 'gods'.

Finally, we were the chosen ones and, scooping Daisy off the floor, in we toddled. The children we left in the waiting room, along with their parents, looked so relieved we were leaving them – can't think why!

I must point out at this time, that my husband Nick is quite, how can I put it, blunt. He is very forthright and says things how they are without always thinking how it might sound to others. Sometimes, this doesn't always go down too well with godlike members of society.

However, as I said, in we went plonking Daisy on the floor. A pleasant, smiley lady, who was clearly clinging onto a past hippy life, was on her throne waiting to quiz.

Handshakes and pleasantries over, we sat like nervous schoolchildren in front of the head teacher. Immediately, the torturous interview began. Did I have a normal pregnancy? Had I taken any medication? Was Daisy ever dropped on her head – WHAT? Really?

On and on the questions continued. Each question being repeated in different guises. In the meantime, Daisy had shuffled her way across the room and sat quite content plucking the hairs on the hippie's legs. Noticing this really put me off my line of thought. I couldn't remove Daisy from the scene of intense plucking, as this would draw attention to the fact I was aware of Daisy's antics.

How embarrassing. Both Nick and I, after exchanging glances, just hoped she'd stop. Miss Hippy was brushing her leg (brushing with her hand not a comb) and continually crossing and uncrossing her legs. She was clearly uncomfortable and trying in vain to stop my little cherub from giving her a complete leg depilation.

Eventually, I had to intervene. It was becoming too uncomfortable and I no longer had any idea of the questions I was being asked. Daisy was hoiked onto my lap in the pretence she may need a snack. I had prepared well for this event, I wanted to appear to be mother earth. No shite was being given to my little petal.

Out came the little box of raisins and crunchy apple sliced and peeled. My, what a perfect mother I was. Daisy showed her disgust by hurling the fruit around the room like little shots of shellfire. Fuck it, my cover was blown and out came the chocolate buttons instead. Content, we all continued.

Miss Hippy, in a low sympathetic voice, told us she had received a report from Worzel that showed worrying signs of severe developmental delay. According to the scientifically conducted horse and comb test, Daisy had a mental age of eight months.

I sat and listened, but wasn't too upset. That's not too bad I thought, her father can't be measuring much more than that – no, I jest!

Miss Hippy continued. Daisy would need an **MRI** scan to see if there were any physiological reasons for her problems. Other specialists would be in touch in the meantime to assist with her development.

Two hours and one leg pluck later, we left feeling a little perplexed and wondering what awaited us around the corner.

Chapter Five
24 Months

Daisy was now mobile. Nightmare! No longer were the bruises confined to her head. Every inch of her body was covered. It was as if she felt no pain, because she never cried when she hit a piece of furniture with any part of her body. She just continued to her destination, taking tables, chairs and bits of wall with her as she went.

She still put everything in her mouth and this was becoming a problem. She liked to chew the corners of our wooden kitchen table after she'd head-butted them. She also had a taste for poo, and would scoop the contents of her nappy out from behind her and sit peacefully enjoying every morsel. You had to be quick to get to the poo before she could. Well, it was one less feed, I suppose!

One sunny day, while I was enjoying a nice cup of tea in my well-tended garden – courtesy of the hubby (his escape from our mad house) – I sat half-arsed observing Daisy between sun-soaking my not-so-perfect-anymore body. I thought she was quiet and content just lolling about on the grass, then from a squint behind my sunglasses I noticed something sticking out of her mouth.

'Daisy,' I called, but to be honest I could have shouted 'Bin Laden' and got the same reaction – nothing! I prised myself up from heaven and grudgingly edged towards her, not expecting to see the horror show awaiting me. Inside Daisy's mouth was a baby bird. Yes, a real baby bird!

Head first, scrawny little legs poking out of pink, dribble-soaked lips. Jesus, what was I to do? If I pulled it would she would bite the head off? What if she swallowed it, how would I explain the episode to all those professionals? *Quavers*, I thought, *they always come to the rescue.*

Out I came, holding Quaver in outstretched hand for the exchange of gifts. She's a clever little bugger at times and managed to put the Quaver in her mouth alongside Tweetie Pie.

Hmm, Tickles. So there I was, lying on the perfectly manicured lawn outside my perfect house, trying to get a bird (presumably dead by now), out of my beautiful princess' mouth. How did I get here? Tweetie came out during an exchange of handfuls of Quavers.

Urgh, I never did like birds since seeing Alfred Hitchcock's film, but Quaver-dribbled, grass-stained dead ones are particularly gross! I threw it on the grass with a shriek. Daisy sat quietly finishing off her crisps unfazed, unaware. Should I take her to hospital? Jesus, what would I say? Could she get bird flu?

I sat staring at her, staring at the dead bird with the Quaver stuck to its beak. Bloody hell! I made a decision. This was best dealt with in secret, at home, where no one would judge and no one would know. And so there it was, the bird was thrown into a hedge, I bleached my hands and Daisy was disinfected to within an inch of her life. No one would ever know! It was our secret.

Chapter Six
Three

Danger Girl, as we had now re-named Daisy, looked like a war zone. Her head was covered in lumps and bruises from her constant head-butting.

I was at my wits end. No professional (why do we call them that?) gave a damn. 'Just make the house safe', I was told. What was I to do? Knock down the walls and replace them with bloody foam pillars? Why did I even bother to consult advice from general practitioners and the like?

It was around this time that Daisy and I had the 'pleasure' of meeting Mother Theresa (name changed to spare blushes), our Portage representative. Now if you don't know what Portage is, as I didn't, let me explain.

A do-gooder comes to your home and teaches you how to play with your child for one hour a week. They observe you while you interact with your child and advise on why your child is obviously failing in their development due to your incredible lack of parenting skills. It wasn't mentioned that my older child Harvey was bright, chopsy and articulate.

Did I talk to Daisy? Did I sit and enjoy a book with her? Jesus, I couldn't even read a bloody newspaper without it being eaten by her! Arghh, I hated this intruder in my house.

She continued every week, bringing stupid crappy boxes

of the same sort of objects Worzel had presented, thrusting them at Daisy who didn't even notice if Mother Theresa was there or not. Daisy always acted in the same nonchalant way. She couldn't care less who was in our house. She took absolutely no notice of them and just sat head-butting, whining or placing anything that would fit into her mouth. If only Mother T would fit.

After a couple of months of absolutely no miracle being performed, Mother Theresa decided it would be a good idea to introduce Daisy to the joys of felt tip pens. Was this women for real? She enthusiastically erected an easel in my kitchen and smoothed a huge sheet of paper on said easel.

Daisy took no notice. I had to encourage Daisy into Mother T's direction by teasing her with food, placing a trail which she hoovered up into her mouth, whilst making her way to her art debut.

Daisy was given her first pen. I must stress at this point, that both the nursery and I had obviously tried to get Daisy to experience the pleasure of scribbling, all to no avail. Each time met with dramatic arm flinging and avoidance. Mother T was getting very excited.

'Ooh, look, she's holding it. Daisy, draw on paper.'

At that command, the pen (red) was inserted into Daisy's mouth.

'No,' Mother T hissed, dropping her guard for a split second.

'Let's try a blue pen. Daisy, copy me.'

Peeling open Daisy's hand to hold the pen was a feat in itself. I could see Mother T's calm exterior slowly unravelling. This was getting quite entertaining. Daisy now had a blue and

21

red tinged mouth.

'We'll try one more time, Mum,' she turned to me and said, noticing that I had a smirk that wouldn't rid itself from my face. This time, Mother T frantically scribbled huge bloody circles on the crisp paper that enveloped the easel. *What a waste of paper*, I thought.

She grabbed Daisy's hand and forced the pen, green this time, into a non-compliant grasp. The horns popped out and Daisy launched the pen into the air. Unbelievably, the pen hit the paper and about a quarter inch splodge was embedded onto the sheet.

'Yippee,' enthused Mother T, circling the splodge. 'Daisy's first mark on a piece of paper.' She even bloody dated it!

She presented me with Daisy's, what she called, 'first of many' pieces of artwork. Mother T left that day looking like a cat that had got the cream. Her chest all proud and protruding, she had the result she'd expected and her work was done!

I know this is quite naughty but I kept making excuses so Mother T could not enthuse herself upon us too much. The weekly visits quickly became monthly and slowly fizzled out. We didn't need her support, I wasn't failing. Daisy was just, well, Daisy. So I'd lost my place in Heaven, but I guess I'd never really secured a place anyway.

Chapter Seven
The Photo Shoot

Like all 'normal' families, I wanted to have some professional photos taken, you know the type, trendy studio, quirky poses, bank robbing costs. I had forewarned the studio that Daisy wasn't your average three-year-old and that she probably wouldn't follow any instructions.

'It's fine,' came the response, 'we see all kinds of children in our studios.'

'Yeah right,' I said under my breath, 'We will see.'

To get Nick to even agree to the shoot was, in itself, a miracle but to get him to wear the jeans, white t-shirt, no socks look (we all wore similar) was a bigger task than getting Daisy to look clean. Anyhow, he did as he was told and moaned and moaned and moaned...

Wait till you see the bill, I thought. He had no idea!

In we trotted, off come our shoes and off Daisy went like a fizzy whippet. Licking a few walls, the floor, then settling down in a corner by a coat someone had hung up that had a furry collar, meow.

The photographer set up her props, a crate, some large balls, you know the sort of thing, and then instructed us to get onto the white shiny floor. Nick did as he was told, Harvey followed, but Daisy had other ideas. Meow, meow, meow,

meow and on it went. I told the photographer to just take photos of Harvey and Nick, but she insisted we had plenty of time and so out came my bag of bribes; a *Barney* book, a *Fimbles* toy, a *Teletubbies* toy, and Quavers (of course). Nothing bloody worked. It was suggested we try and play a game with Daisy so there we are, all chasing each other on the shiny floor like bloody nutters, Daisy just ignored us all. Meow.

I'd had enough, sweating and filled with anxiety my guard came down out of both frustration and being pissed off with my abnormal life. I grabbed Daisy's hand, whipped her off the floor and slid her at speed across the shiny floor; my god she sped across that floor like a curling ball on ice. Please stop before you hit the wall I muttered under my breath, she did, just. Crikey, she was not impressed and lay on the floor like a rag doll.

'OK, Harvey,' shouted the photographer, 'Lie next to Daisy.'

Skidding across the floor on his knees Harvey did as he was told and got an almighty whack off Daisy.

Click, click, click went the camera. *Brutal*, I thought.

'Right, Mum, Dad, get on the floor.' Click, click, click.

This is going to be disastrous, I thought. And a bloody expensive disaster at that.

'Barney book... NOW,' screamed the photographer. Nick threw the book like a missile, Daisy lifted it (upside down). Click, click.

Ten minutes passed in a whirl. I just wanted to pack up and leave, exhausted, upset, angry, deflated. Harvey, on the other hand, was amazing and made my heart melt, he was so good with Daisy and really tried his utmost to make her look the photographers way. Such a kind boy.

Amazingly we had some fabulous photos. Not your average family portraits but nevertheless great shots. When we finally left you could see the photographer slump, she earned the extortionate fee.

Chapter Eight

Speech and Language

Speech and Language specialists were now on-board the funny bus as well. A lovely lady visited every week and, to be fair, was very well-meaning, but her strategies were not really geared for a child like mine. No one's were.

Bubble blowing, picture exchange cards and copy cat games just didn't wash with Daisy. The bubble blowing was a disaster. Daisy would just get frustrated and smash the blower into Lovely Lady's face, often dislodging her glasses.

Picture exchange again was a no-no. This simple method of communication is called PECS (Picture Exchange Communication System). It is for the child to hand over a picture of the item they require.

For example, a cup/beaker picture would mean they wanted a drink. A picture of an apple would mean they wanted, you got it, an apple. Daisy couldn't grasp this, and on the limited times she paid any attention, she just tried to eat the laminated picture – not ideal!

Lovely Lady worked tirelessly with us for about six months, then could do no more. Her good intentions were well-meaning, but fruitless. No one was making any progress. None of the professionals to date could quite fathom Daisy. Daisy was different, very different.

Chapter Nine
The Psychologist (Part One)

W hy did I allow these people to invade my home? They were more loopy than they were insinuating Daisy was. The latest uninvited specialist was a peculiar species. A psychologist, man, woman, difficult to tell, but due to the introduction I was guessing the latter.

She was accompanied by our old friend Mother Theresa, who gloated as she recalled her 'success' at getting Daisy to 'draw'. She truly did have a vivid imagination. I sat there nodding in a 'can't be bothered to even react' type of manner. I wonder what they thought of me?

She/he, for want of a better name, studied studiously every move of Daisy while scratching notes in her diary. It was difficult to keep Daisy in the room, as she was showing no signs of being at all interested in the array of new tests that were being targeted her way.

By now, Daisy was only really interested in flicking the pages of books. Any book really, but particularly the Argos catalogue, as the pages ripped nice and easily. She would sit for an eternity, concentrating on each turning page studying the upside down scripts. If you dared to interrupt a page turn you would risk injury, so it was always best to allow the ritual to.run its course.

She/he didn't listen when I'd warned her of this. Whack! A full-on Hollywood smack straight into She/he's face ensued. Why don't these people listen? I always forewarn guests to be on their guard. More scribbles followed into the 'little black book'. Unbelievably, She/he started asking Daisy questions

'Hello, Daisy, you're so pretty. What's your favourite toy? What noise does a cat make? How old are you? Where's Mummy?'

Daisy sat there eating a piece of old food she'd found under the leg of the sofa. No reaction, nothing. Just content munching, while I pretended not to notice. She/he scribbled. Scribbled a lot, looking at Daisy sympathetically, puzzled. Studying, staring.

'We'll be in touch with our report.'

They left, scratching their heads, muttering as they scurried up the drive, then drove off in the beat up Fiesta they'd dared to park outside my house. What would the neighbours think? The shame!

A follow-up appointment arrived with Miss Hippy. Nick, Daisy and I dutifully attended, hopeful that some questions could be answered. By now, I had tried to diagnose Daisy myself. Surely she was autistic? I had become an expert on the subject. I should have been the spokesperson for the National Autistic Society. Daisy was autistic, it was obvious. She had all the signs. Well, nearly all the signs:-

No Purposeful Play
No Social Awareness
In her own world
Does not show interest

I presented my diagnosis to Miss Hippy. She disagreed. Hmmm! In her mind, Daisy was presenting severe learning difficulties. What the hell did that mean? Miss Hippy was prepared to refer Daisy to another team of specialists. Christ, the world is crawling with them. Who would be better able to dispel my theory that Daisy was autistic? Nick just sat there. I don't even know if he was awake for the appointment. Oh hang on, he must have been, because he did make some smart-arse remark about my theory, then another comment that completely discredited Miss Hippy's work.

We awaited the specialists consultation, leaving the room as we always did, exhausted and confused by being no closer to an answer, if indeed there ever would be an answer.

It wasn't long before we faced the multi-disciplinary team who knew it all. It annoys me that they chat about you for a good half hour before you ever go into these consultations. Who knows what pre-conceived opinion they then have?

In we walked, happy that Daisy was no longer trying to knock the huge fish tank off its feet by hitting it with a large ride on car in the waiting area. We were hopeful that finally, we may find out what was wrong with Daisy.

There must have been ten people in the room. Each sat on couches or chairs of differing heights that circled the room. It was quite daunting, but nothing worried Daisy.

The meeting began.

Each person in turn, clockwise around the room, introduced themselves. Their qualifications ranged from Consultant Paediatrician to Office Cleaner – well nearly. The contents of the Early Learning Centre was strewn in a manner that suggested they were looking for Daisy to 'play nicely'.

Instead, Daisy kicked each toy around the room with a real sense of malice. She then proceeded to lick every surface in the room. Taps, shoes, chairs, legs, phone – you name it, it got a good licking. After licking, she threw a phone and then crumpled up any paper she could grab from the desk. She just didn't want to play, or didn't know how to.

During *Question Time*, I tried to ignore Daisy's behaviour and proceeded to 'start at the beginning' telling the tale from conception. Not all the juicy details, though. Nick was in a bit of a mood. He hated being in a room full of so-called experts. He had no respect for any of them and at any opportunity quipped in with a sarcastic one-liner that would be brushed aside.

Each professional had their own set of questions, each asked with head tilted to one side and sympathetic mouths. One, however, stuck out. I'd noticed her giving me daggers from the very start and knew she'd be trouble. She was a very short, dumpy, back-of-the-queue-when-they-gave-out-looks creature.

She blurted out that the whole meeting was a waste of time, as there was, and I quote, 'clearly nothing wrong with Daisy. She just needs a bit of help with her speech.'

We were dumfounded. I immediately mentally named her Gobshite. Her genius findings were concluded, because her neighbour's son was the same age as Daisy and he too couldn't speak. We couldn't believe what we were hearing, it was awkward and embarrassing. We were made to feel like we were wasting their time.

Nick questioned whether her neighbour's son licked all surfaces, ate poo and made no attempt to communicate, too.

Gobshite just sat and all the other clowns agreed in nodding unison.

'Daisy is not autistic,' they told us. 'We'll follow up in a year if you have any concerns, but we believe she's just a little delayed.'

A YEAR!

Arghhhhhh! We were ushered from the room ashamed, angry and upset. I believe I did lose it at this point and swore some obscenity at Gobshite, which probably didn't help our cause, but made me feel better.

I didn't speak to Nick for hours, he hadn't been very supportive in my opinion, but Nick saw Daisy's condition in a different light to me, we would sort this together. The case would continue.

Chapter Ten
Nursery

Daisy had attended the same nursery since she was fourteen weeks old. It was expensive, but well worth the 'me time' it gave. Harvey was there as well and had been since it first opened. The staff were very good. Harvey was as bright as a button and very popular. Daisy had her very own, very expensive one-to-one – enough said!

When Daisy reached the age of three, staff started to avoid me when I dropped her and Harvey off (at one minute past eight) and picked them up (at one minute to six). I caught their awkward glances and was waiting for the inevitable conversation – they could no longer have Daisy in the nursery. I knew it would come and I understood, but I was still angry and bitter.

After gaining advice from a very knowledgeable and good friend I decided that the Local Education Authority would be my next port-of-call. Oh my, what a minefield.

Chapter Eleven
The LEA

If you ever have the unfortunate task of having to deal with the Local Education Authority (LEA), then my heart and best wishes go out to you. It's a bloody nightmare! Obviously the people who work there are just doing a job, but Jesus, they don't half make sure they go by the bloody book.

To get any help whatsoever, Daisy needed to have a Statement of Educational Needs, or be 'Statemented' for short. We'd never come across this term, so had no idea what a horrendous journey we were about to embark on.

Forms. No, not forms. Huge bloody empty scripts started landing at our feet. Endless hours were spent repeating ourselves over what Daisy could, or couldn't (to be more precise), do.

We dutifully filled the pages with all the information the 'powers that be' could possibly need to know. Days turned into weeks of form filling, each time constantly repeating what was previously written. My theory was, that the 'powers that be' were trying to trip us up. At the slightest slip of the pen, we'd be thrust back to the beginning until we submitted defeat and disappeared off their radar. Oh no, not us, we were here to stay!

To cut a ridiculously lengthy story short, it took a visit to

Head Honcho at the LEA to get anywhere, as we were just being constantly fobbed off. Nick, Daisy and myself took a little uninvited trip to her lair and basically ambushed her.

Head Honcho agreed to speak to us, probably because Daisy was causing such a kerfuffle in the corridors of power. Inside her incredibly untidy room, Head Honcho sat slowly turning the carefully scripted pages I'd spent many a night compiling whilst sipping delicately at a glass of the old vino. Anyone who knows me will know this is a complete lie and I would've been gulping volumes of the great white grape.

Meanwhile, Daisy was getting restless and we could no longer appease her with food, so her wrecking spree thus began. Papers went flying, files flew, the phone lines were yanked. Honcho must have panicked slightly. What if we held her hostage? I did wonder if she had a panic button. If she did, no one bothered coming.

'What is it you want?' she questioned.

'HELP,' we answered.

Honcho listened almost sympathetically and, maybe just to rid herself of us, agreed we needed 'special schooling'. NO, not me and Nick... Daisy! She would be in touch.

Chapter Twelve
The Special School

Now this is going to sound awful, but my first visit to a 'special school' filled me with utter horror. No way was it the type of school my gorgeous little girl needed to attend.

The children there weren't like Daisy. They looked different. They dressed different. They smelt different. They *were* different. Daisy wouldn't fit in. Daisy wasn't *that* bad – was she? Maybe we'd got it wrong. Oh my God, what had I got us into? Was I turning Daisy into a child she wasn't? Perhaps I did have Munchausen by Proxy – crikey!

I was in a daze walking around the school looking at the poor, poor children. My heart wanted to break. Not just for them, but for me as well. Daisy didn't need this type of environment. She might turn into one of them. Oh no, this wasn't right, not right for my baby girl.

I tried to act pleasant in front of the teachers/carers at the school asking bloody stupid questions like: 'Are the children happy here?' and 'Do they learn much?'

Jesus, my mind was spinning. I'd never come across children so severely disabled. Was this where they were hidden away from society?

Wheelchairs lined the corridors, seating contraptions were everywhere you turned, there were nurses on site to feed the tube fed children, and strange noises echoed the walls. A pupil here and there would pass me and stroke my hair or hang off my arm. NO! This was not a suitable place for my angel – was it?

I left feeling physically sick, taking home with me a prospectus with pictures of the pupils on the front. Even that filled me with a sense of angst. These poor children looked so odd, so strange, not like my little petal.

At home, I sat staring at the booklet and the pictures in it. Why was I so selfish? Why did I think Daisy was better than these children? Their parents didn't choose to have a disabled child, just like I hadn't counted on having 'a Daisy'.

I waited and waited for Nick to come home from work and left the prospectus on the table. I tried to sound positive. It was a lovely school and all the staff had been so friendly and caring, but I didn't have to convince Nick. As soon as he looked at the front cover of the prospectus he proclaimed that no way was his daughter going to a school like that!

We sat in silence.

I don't think it really hit us until then as to how bad Daisy was. Or was she? Sure, we knew she was unique, we knew she was different, but we really hadn't bargained on her needing the type of institution now being suggested.

Had we forced this upon ourselves? Crap!

Chapter Thirteen
Three Years Six Months

The Statement of Educational Needs landed on the doormat... thud! This was it, this was reality. Daisy *was* 'different'. I must have read and re-read it a hundred times, but it didn't get any easier. Actually reading what help your child needed in school was a hard pill to swallow.

That August, just like any other proud mother, I went to buy all of her school essentials. Grey pinafore, red shirt and cardigan, white socks and patent shoes. I loved how cute she looked. She always stood out as being very, very beautiful, but behind my proud eyes were tears. Many, many tears at the realization that my little girl was different.

The first few months of school went very well. Daisy was always happy to attend. Well, to be honest, she didn't have a clue she was at school, she just enjoyed the attention she was getting. It was only when we started getting messages home from school telling us what she had 'achieved', that our suspicions were roused.

Surely Daisy couldn't do *all* the things the school were saying she could without showing any sign of these achievements at home? Every day, more and more achievements, and both Nick and I were confused. Either Daisy was the master of deception and the school teachers had performed a miracle, or the school were telling fibs. We arranged to meet.

The staff in Daisy's class were lovely, caring people, but I think they tried to make us feel better by 'bigging up' Daisy's abilities. This was a mistake. I had, for the last two years, tried to educate people about the fact that Daisy was different. She didn't fit any boxes. She couldn't talk, think, understand cues, understand commands, or understand full stop! How, all of a sudden, could she build a tower, press a button, and tidy up her toys?

Trying hard not to criticise, Nick and I listened to her teacher, who enthused as to what Daisy could now do. While she spoke, I kept a sly eye on what she was actually doing in the corner of the room – she had tipped a chair upside down and was trying to eat the leg!

Finally, after listening for far too long, Nick had had enough and asked the teacher if she could video Daisy doing these activities.

'Oh no, that's not legal,' came the reply. 'It's against Daisy's human rights!'

'OK, well could you get Daisy to demonstrate her new-found skills in front of us?' Nick asked. We were willing to be corrected.

The teacher called her over and of course Daisy continued to chew on the chair leg. Nick went over to Daisy and removed her from her snack. She wasn't happy and tried to head-butt him, but he just calmly smiled.

Placing her in front of some bricks, he asked the teacher to persuade her to build the tower. We knew it was never going to happen, nor the pressing of a button, nor the tidying of the toys.

Defeated, the teacher held up her hands and had to admit it was their aim that Daisy would do the tasks set sooner rather than later, but as yet, just hurled items like missiles. The school liked to put positive thoughts to parents, as a way of encouraging skills at home. I call them fibs!

Phew, we were relieved. Not because we wanted Daisy to be naughty – if that's even the right term – but simply because we wanted others to see that she was so very different. That our Daisy was unique.

We didn't expect what happened next. We were just getting on with managing Daisy the best we could. After all, there was nothing really wrong with her. Although apparently, following the meeting four months earlier, opinions clashed and Daisy was the topic of many discussions. Letters requesting appointments started arriving in the post on a daily basis.

Appointments took up all of my time and I felt like no one understood what I was trying to tell them about Daisy. The specialists listened while scribbling notes, but they didn't offer any help. Surely there must be others like Daisy? After each appointment, I left feeling alone with a truly unique child. Was I the only one who knew she was *so* different? Why couldn't anyone else see it?

I started to distance myself from everyone who ever asked about Daisy because they usually ended the conversation with, 'Oh, isn't she coming on.'

And all I ever wanted to scream was, 'NO, SHE'S NOT BLOODY "COMING ON", NOW PISS OFF!'

Invites to 'friends' parties started to diminish. Probably

partly to do with me being so cold towards any Daisy related questions, and partly to do with the fact that Daisy would attack any child or parent who came near her.

Mothers would twitter in huddled corners glancing over from time to time. I became extremely paranoid that the whole world thought I was a really bad mother who had allowed their child to cause death and destruction wherever she roamed.

Children were absolutely terrified of Daisy. She was, after all, big for her age with a lot of strength behind her. Kids would be running, screeching before she even laid a finger on them. I often wished she'd clip some of the lovely little monsters who hadn't given her a chance.

I got sick of saying sorry to the planet and decided it was now just me, my family and Daisy. No one else mattered.

Chapter Fourteen
The Gym

The crèche at the local leisure club was always full whenever I tried to book Daisy in for an hour – funny that – so I only ever took her with me when Nick and Harvey went for a swim. It sounds so simple, doesn't it? Take your children for a nice leisurely swim and end the day with a spot of dinner. It was never like that for us.

The whole scenario was a complete trauma for me. I would attempt to change Daisy into swim nappies on a plastic changing mat, her head and legs hanging over each end, table legs warping under the strain and feeding her crisps to keep her content.

Daisy would be fighting me, making her strange noises. Mothers and their cherubs would try not to stare, but find it too much of a temptation not to 'watch the show'. Once into her huge swim nappies, Daisy would escape and often bring me gifts that she had pilfered from open lockers: shampoo bottles, hairbrushes and once she even brought me a nice pair of pre-worn knickers in her mouth!

I'd mastered the art of changing into my swimsuit in less than thirty seconds, so that I could scoop Daisy out of someone's locker and take her to 'enjoy' her swim. Nick and Harvey, relaxed as ever, then had to endure the pleasure of the 'whale attack', while I would dream of being a normal family.

Our rule used to be that by the time the third child was crying we should leave the pool. So six minutes later I usually had my clothes back on and was snapped back into my abnormal world. I had the great job of then re-dressing Shamu and ordering lunch, while I left behind an uneasy dressing room full of staring strangers.

One day in particular that stands out was when I allowed Daisy to roam free while I was ordering some lunch. I stupidly must have believed that for a split second she was fine to wander off. After all, most kids there would be sheltered by their parents as soon as they caught a sniff of Daisy in their radar.

I sort of felt something brewing in the background, but wasn't really 'with it', if you know what I mean? Suddenly, my little darling in her beautiful petal laden dress, charged past me meowing (a sound you'll soon realise is one of her favourites).

I didn't really pay much attention, until I noticed she was being pursued by a rather red-faced man. I stopped ordering food and called Daisy sternly thinking some paedophile had taken a fancy to her. I don't know why I bothered calling her, she never responded to my motherly tones. Then I noticed brown marks down her pretty frock.

Oh no, I thought. *Please, God, don't say she's pooped!*

Nope, she hadn't, it was a sort of thick peppery gravy? From out of nowhere, abuse started being thrown towards me from the red-faced man (who quite frankly should have spent a bit more time on the exercise bike instead of eating in the restaurant).

'Is *she* yours?' he questioned. I wanted to say no. 'She's taken my bloody steak!'

'What? No!'

'YEESSSS!'

Daisy had taken this red-faced-man's steak off his plate, just as he was tucking in. What would you have done? The same as me? I took the steak off Daisy (after a bit of a fight) and handed it back to him.

This was a mistake, he was FURIOUS. He just sort of stared at me and then at the steak for what seemed like a lifetime. Daisy did try to take the steak back off him, so at this point I decided to leave quickly, rushing past the sniggering audience with Daisy meowing and protesting in my arms.

'Sorry, so sorry.'

Sometime later, Nick and Harvey appeared in the car park with questioning expressions on their faces. They knew not to ask what was wrong. They knew I was about to explode.

Daisy, sucking on her tasty gravy fingers, had no idea. No clue as to what she had done. What was I going to do with her?

43

Chapter Fifteen
Hospital

Things were starting to get tough. Daisy would constantly bang her head on the hardest surface she could find; floors, tables, walls (usually the corners to get a bigger hit). I'd been to the doctor, but I may as well have just talked to the bruises on Daisy's head, 'cos no one listened!

Daisy seemed to be unwell quite a lot of the time too. I didn't know what it was, but she just wasn't quite right. With constant high temperatures and being very hard to wake, we went through weeks of reluctant visits to the doctor. Looking back, I don't know what I was thinking taking her while enduring the scrutinising and raised eyebrows, because I never got any answers. Maybe they thought I was a rubbish mother who had Munchausen by Proxy?

The final crunch came when typically, on a day I was at work (yes, amazingly throughout all this I worked part-time in a hospital!) and both grannies were looking after Daisy, she became quite ill again. Over the phone, I advised them to get a cab and take Daisy to the doctor's and I'd meet them there.

So, they duly took Daisy. After a battle with the receptionist – you know what I mean – Daisy, unconscious by now, was seen by what only can be described as a 'just out of nappies' GP.

Guess what? Daisy had that all too familiar 'virus' that everyone gets when a doctor has no idea what is wrong with their patient. Still semi-conscious, Daisy was then given Calpol by the doctor, which, due to her lack of consciousness, was immediately thrown back up. This was the point at which I entered the room (I've always had impeccable timing).

I thought my head was going to explode. I demanded the doctor arrange for Daisy to be seen by someone who could at least be served in a pub and off we all went to hospital. OH MY GOD!

The grannies were panicking, I was cursing, we couldn't bloody park, and then none of us had any change for the machine. Sod it! I just abandoned the car and lifted a still unconscious Daisy out – weighing a ton and stinking of sick. Our entourage battled through the wall of smoke and fluffy slippers that you always seem to get outside a hospital entrance, and made our way to the Children's Unit.

The staff in the unit were fantastic and within no time at all Daisy was hooked up to all sorts of machinery. I suddenly felt that maybe, just maybe, someone would now listen to me. Then my world came crashing down.

Alarms starting sounding, things were bleeping, staff were running about and my baby was FITTING. Doctors came from everywhere, a bit like that saying about buses.

Daisy was blue. She was stiff. I thought she was dead. I'd never seen anyone have a seizure before and boy was I terrified. The curtains were pulled like you see on the telly, but I was in this awful production. Shaking, silently hysterical, feeling very alone in a very dark place, I felt numb. I'm unsure about the timing as it was a blur, but sometime later, my

45

darkness was lifted and I heard the words, 'Mum, she's fine. Come and hold her hand.'

Daisy, my most special, beautiful little girl was OK. She was asleep and pink again. God was she beautiful. I cried like I had never cried before.

That was the start of many, many stays in hospital. Each stay was an experience. Each stay I'd have to explain over and over again why Daisy couldn't talk, why she wore nappies, why she had no understanding. Surely there were other children like my Daisy, surely?

They say a positive always results from a negative and you could say Daisy showing an actual physical ailment, helped her father become her daddy. Nick started to show an emotion towards Daisy that I had never seen before. He held her when she had fits, he held her when she didn't. He started to love her. He really did start to care.

It made me share her much more. She didn't just belong to me anymore, as I'd so selfishly thought, she belonged to all of us. Her family pet name became Roo (she bounced about like Little Roo from *Winnie the Pooh*) and we started to love and laugh again. Roo made us laugh. Roo was funny.

Chapter Sixteen

Four

What's the saying, it never rains it pours? Our happy family didn't last long. Daisy was having seizures regularly. Sometimes fifteen in any one day, at least on one day of each week. Each time I thought she was going to die. I would sit beside her holding her, thinking each one would be her last. I thought of nothing else. Nick and Harvey didn't exist. I abandoned them and only Daisy mattered. Time moved slowly.

Then the medication started kicking in. Fits were roughly every two to three weeks, but nevertheless, they were tiresome and all my energy was zapped. Daisy was sleeping less and less during the night. Waking at two, then three. How are you supposed to function as a mother, as a wife?

My mirror image was not good. Was I selfish worrying about my own reflection?

Other professions started jumping on the bandwagon. They all wanted a slice of the pie. ENT, Ophthalmics, the appointments were endless, horrible. Neurology became involved and all the tests one would expect start to escalate.

Overnights in hospital became too frequent for my liking. I hated my life, this was not how it was supposed to be. It wasn't what I signed up for on that beach in Mauritius.

Speech and Language, Paediatricians, they all wanted a say but none of them had any answers. None of them talked to each other, none of them really cared once the door had closed behind us.

I felt like a broken record, all I ever said was the same thing over and over again: 'What's wrong with Daisy?' No one ever answered. No one had an answer.

It was at the age of four that we started to notice yet another problem. A squint. This added to my worry. Daisy was referred to an ophthalmologist and, to our astonishment, an appointment came within days of the referral. Was this significant we wondered?

It was yet another appointment I would need to take time off work for. I was getting more and more short tempered when new consultants always ended up asking the same monotonous questions right back to conception. This, I believe, is a major failing in our National Health Service (NHS). So much time is wasted repeating yourself. All relevant information should be added to patient notes on one multi-discipline page. OK, rant over!

This consultant was a fabulous little Italian man. He was tiny and I did fear Daisy could floor him if he got too close. I'd already warned every parent and child in the waiting room that Daisy wasn't in a great mood and caution should be taken when coming within metres of her, but as happens almost on a daily basis, no one ever listens. This day was no exception.

We were called into a ridiculously small room for a consultation. Daisy was trying to escape from her buggy but, luckily for me, did not have the intelligence to try and release the strap. I knew we were relatively safe to proceed with the consultation, but I did reiterate several times my warning that she was not in a good mood.

Mr Little began. He started by quietly reading her notes, thick notes. He didn't speak much. Smiled, but didn't speak. He then took a thin stick with a dog on the end – not a real dog – out of a drawer. He slowly moved it in front of Daisy's eyes, but he was far too close. The little dog was too close. Snatch. Daisy's reaction time has always amazed me.

Daisy now had the dog and stick in between her teeth. Mr Little flinched backwards in his black leather swivel chair. Carefully holding one end, he tried to remove it from the jaws of my cherub. Nah, that baby was staying put. At the risk of removing Daisy's teeth, Mr Little decided to carry on the appointment without the dog stick. So, stupidly, out of the TARDIS drawer came a stick with – drum roll – an elephant on it.

Just re-read the last paragraph and replace dog with elephant, for that was what happened next. Daisy threw the dog stick across the room, keeping the dog in her mouth but now had an elephant stick to accompany her friend. I knew not to try to take her new-found possessions from her. I knew to just sit and smile and say, 'Just give her a little while and she'll soon get bored.' I knew full well I was talking bollocks.

No more sticks came out that day, in fact nothing much was done that day. I would have to return in two weeks and do it all again. Great!

Two weeks later sat in the clinic repeating to lucky mothers that they should be careful their children didn't get too close, was a real heart sinking moment.

I was so tired of mums staring over magazines, old people glaring disapprovingly and children almost in awe of the destruction Daisy could cause in a waiting room – tip chairs, throw toys and papers, pull posters off walls – and all with no real telling off. I would just follow her, scooping up her mess. What's the point of a telling off if the person you're aiming it at can't understand a bloody word or gesture you're sending them? I no longer had the energy to waste.

Mr Little swooned into clinic in the only way consultants can. There is an air of superiority that surrounds them. Now I know why Nick has problems with them. Anyhow, he was very nice again and this time didn't attempt the dog/elephant stick trick. No, this time, it was cut to the chase. He would like to perform a procedure on Daisy – Botox!

Bloody hell, she's only four, I thought. *I know celebs are having the procedure at a younger age but four is a bit too young!*

He explained a small incision would be made in the corner of her eye and Botox would be injected. This would make the muscles relax and the squint would be repaired. Simple.

I was desperate to ask if I could have any remainder for my crows feet, but kept quiet. Maybe I could ask closer to the time?

It would require a general anaesthetic. Oh jeez, not again. Thoughts went back to a year earlier when Daisy had one for an MRI scan. Nick held her top half and I held her bottom half, whilst an anaesthetist tried to gas her. She was so strong it took ages and was very, very upsetting. Eventually, after looking at me with startled, hysterical eyes, Daisy was grey and out for the count. Nick was slumped in a chair and I thought it was out of exhaustion. No, he had inhaled anaesthetic as well, bloody idiot!

A date was set for the operation. We turned up, it was cancelled. The second date was given. I was so nervous, anxious, but still in the back of my mind wondered if I could have the remaining Botox. Yet again the anaesthetising of Daisy was very traumatic. Rabbit in headlight eyes stared at me and that was just Nick! Anyhow, soon she was under and tear-filled we sat by her bed on the ward to await her return.

We sat, grabbed a coffee, sat again, read a paper, sat once more, clock watched. Time slowed down. After what felt like an eternity, we were called to recovery. Our poor baby. Asleep, but not looking rested. We sat just staring at her then accompanied her back to the ward.

Daisy isn't great after anaesthetic, probably due to her epilepsy, so when she started to come round she was sick and had a little seizure. As usual I panicked, but she was soon in a postictal sleep – the altered state of consciousness after an epileptic seizure – and again we just sat.

A few hours went by and Daisy woke as if nothing had happened, but one thing was clear (or not clear as the case may be) her eye. Oh My God. There was so much blood pooled in her eye and she looked like she'd had a stroke. I was distraught. Nurses called Mr Little and he came to check.

'Fine, yes, everything's fine. Lovely, great, although I think we need to put a patch over her eye to prevent infection for a few days.'

'I don't think she will tolerate that,' I faltered, but was not listened to. A nurse arrived with a big pad and some tape.

Daisy was half asleep, but within seconds made it known she was not happy. Slap. One unhappy nurse. The pad was almost thrown on and I know within seconds it will be off. One, two, three, four seconds later in the mouth went the pad – I knew it!

'She'll be fine, nurse, leave it,' said a disgruntled Mr Little.

Hmmm, I wasn't convinced, but he assured us all was as expected and the drooping face would go within days.

'Don't worry, Mum,' he announced apologetically. Still a huge shock though. Poor Roo, what was I doing to her?

As you will soon discover, I always discharge Daisy well ahead of time every time she visits hospital. What's the point in waiting on a ward, being amongst all sorts of diseases and witnessing numerous shift changes, just to be told after an extra day you can go home? I know when Daisy is OK and I know she's always happier and easier to manage at home, so home we go.

Discharge papers signed, we made our escape.

Chapter Seventeen
Five

The seizures increased again and my sleep became very disturbed as I would lie next to Daisy just waiting for the next one. Medication was switched and added to. I felt so upset having to drug my angel. One saving grace, however, was the introduction of melatonin. WONDER DRUG! It saved my sanity, gave me my evenings back and knocked out my little petal at precisely quarter to seven every night. Heaven!

My administering of medication to Daisy has always looked quite brutal to any onlookers, but I am of the belief that it's better to get it over with quickly rather than prolong the grief. After all, she had to have it, so I had to win. My stance has always been the same, straddle her against the sofa, grip her tight with one hand across her cheeks and squirt. In it goes, twice. Gosh, that sounds a bit pornographic.

Within seconds of my released grip, all is forgotten and Daisy continued as if nothing happened. Told you, she's like a goldfish.

Chapter Eighteen
The Whale

Yet again, another hospital outpatient appointment beckoned. As was the norm now, most appointments I took her to on my own as Nick, quite rightly so, found them an utter waste of time. How many times can a person repeat themselves without resorting to violence?

This appointment was with a consultant neurologist I had met on just a couple of occasions. He was a tall, kind, gentle man and I found him quite shy and unassuming, almost nervous of me. Let's call him Mr Nice. Surprisingly, for a consultant, he was 'normal'. He had sorted out Daisy's medications and helped me understand epilepsy. He found Daisy very intriguing and I liked the fact he seemed to care.

Turning up at the clinic was very familiar. All the staff knew Roo and all seemed to find her amusing. I loved the fact her clothes were always commented on and everyone *always* said how they would kill to have Rapunzel hair like hers.

I felt very flattered. Proud. I liked showing her off. If you didn't know it, you would think she was a completely healthy, 'normal' girl. Sad that looks were very deceiving.

Those bloody fish in the huge tank by reception were always a magnet to Daisy. *One day*, I kept thinking while keeping guard of the tank, *she's definitely going to have it!* With every bash at my ankles of the sit-in toy police car she was pushing, I would wince and clench a fist but NO, I couldn't let her have direct aim.

'Daisy Rainey, Room 4,' a voice called out. Phew, Nemo lived to swim another day.

I was a little surprised to see Miss Hippy sitting with Mr Nice. I wasn't expecting it and wondered why the audience. Miss Hippy sat in silence, sympathetically smiling at me. Eh? I did notice she had trousers on for this meeting with Daisy. I bet she still re-lived the plucking. Mind you, she hadn't covered up her armpits and every now and again I would get a peak of long ginger strands of underarm hair trying to escape her tie-dyed clothing.

Daisy could do a good job there, I thought, *it would keep her busy for hours!*

Mr Nice started. Within moments of him speaking, my brain began to shut down. The more he spoke, the more I was in a fuzzy, heady, blank state. From walking in quite jovially, I now sat as if I'd been struck by a steam train.

I can't tell you what was said, as I think my body's protection system has blotted it out of my memory, but I remembered him saying the words Rett Syndrome and Angelman Syndrome. Words I had never heard before. Words that meant nothing but sounded so significant.

These syndromes were what he wanted to test her for. One of these syndromes could be the answer. Mr Nice briefly described their symptoms, but I was in shock, couldn't take it in.

Numb, I walked out of the clinic with some leaflets. I

walked trance like to the car and kissing Daisy on the forehead, placed her in her car seat. It was a very lonely, long, sad, tearful drive home. I kept looking at her in the rear view mirror, crying, crying and crying some more.

I had arranged for Nick to pick Harvey up from after school club, so when I pulled up on the drive, I was surprised that neither of them were there. The house was empty, my life felt empty. A note on the kitchen table explained all.

Gone to look at a whale stranded on the beach. Won't be long x

Jesus, of all the days I needed someone he was out looking at a dead bloody whale! What's the chances of that happening? I kept looking at Daisy. I longed for her to cuddle me, smile at me, just acknowledge me, but no, she couldn't let me in. I didn't know what to do, my life had just been dealt another blow.

Google came out to play. Rett Syndrome. I became engrossed. It was too much to take in. I convinced myself Mr Nice was right. Yes, yes, that's what she has, OH MY GOD, what would I tell Nick? Angelman Syndrome, oh God my head was spinning, her symptoms match this as well. I sat, I stared, I sobbed, I waited and I waited.

A key turned in the lock. Right, it was time for a brave, smiling face.

'Hi, Harv, tell me all the gross details then,' I enthused.

Harvey was excited. Firstly, because he'd been out late on a school night on the beach, in the dark. Secondly, because Nick had taken him as close as possible to the smelly dead lump of blubber and they'd seen a football being cut out of it's stomach. Was that appropriate? I didn't care, he'd loved it.

For the next two hours I had to snap back to motherhood. Feed, bath, moan, shout, pour a glass of wine. It wasn't until the cherubs were sleeping that Nick asked how the appointment had gone. I slugged my wine, tears welling up in my eyes. I couldn't speak, so handed him the two leaflets I'd been given.

Through sobbing tones, I murmured our special beautiful innocent child may have one of these dreadful syndromes. What happened next really shook my world. I have never, ever seen Nick cry and I never want to see it again. It was deep, raw and broke me. We sat in silence. We wanted to hold each other, but we just couldn't.

Chapter Nineteen

Six

At the age of about six, it was decided by Mr Nice that Daisy would require a lumbar puncture to obtain some spinal fluid to test for something or other.

To be honest, she has been tested for so many things over the years that I have no recollection of what the procedure was for. All I know is that it was another anaesthetic, another hospital stay, more seizures, more stress and more tears.

Was it useful? Was it heck. The sample of fluid taken was contaminated. Doctors wanted to do it all again and rightly, or wrongly, we refused. Waste of time and such a terrible time for my girl.

Chapter Twenty
Social Services

I have been lucky enough to not have grown up ever having any involvement with social services, so when Daisy's health visitor told me that she would be handing over care of duty to social services I was a little bit astonished. You see, to me, social workers only dealt with problem families, mistreated children and the like. Not mothers like me.

I was as good a mother as I could be. OK, I liked the odd glass of wine, but only after half past five in the evening! I had never hit my children - hang on, I tell a lie, I did smack Harvey on the top of the legs once and a few times on the back of his hand. Ah yes, and I once zipped up the skin of his chest while putting him in his sun protection swim top - ouch, but I'd never smacked Daisy. What would be the point?

I was *very* guilty of shouting. Boy can I shout but, for me, this is my release of frustrations. Surely it's better shouting than giving them a thump, so I was a little concerned as to why I was on the list for social services. Very soon a social worker would be visiting.

Very soon came, very soon! My house was spotless, Daisy was spotless. Nick was home, had to be apparently, so he was particularly grumpy even for him. I was dressed like something out of Wisteria Avenue and the coffee was brewing – perfect!

Ding dong (that's not really the sound of my door bell). She'd arrived. She wasn't anything like I'd expected. She was young, pretty, fashionable. The complete opposite to my picture of a social worker; middle-aged, scruffy, no make-up. I warmed to her straight away and Nick soon perked up as well!

Introductions over, Daisy did her usual and ignored Miss Trendy for the first twenty minutes, but then decided to show who's boss. She pushed, shoved, slapped, and then pulled hair until it was getting embarrassing for everyone. Daisy has never liked me talking to people and has always let her feelings be known. Nick decided to take Daisy for a walk so Miss Trendy and I could chat.

Miss Trendy explained why she had been assigned Daisy. Not because of concerns, but because Daisy was Disabled – a term I had never really considered before. She was a disabled children's social worker. Ah, I felt slightly more comfortable – I think.

Miss Trendy continued. She would be able to offer me help with Daisy's care so I could spend more time with Harvey and Nick. She could offer me advice on special needs groups and family supporters. You name it, it seemed to be out there.

I was a little shell shocked. So far it had been just the four of us alone in this minefield of problems and challenges, now we were offered help should we need it. I was left a bundle of literature to wade through and was assured Miss Trendy would be in touch very soon to decide what help we would be offered. Wow!

True to her word, it wasn't long before she got in touch. She would like to bring a lady with her who cared for disabled children in her own home so that parents could have a break. It would start off as daycare breaks with the intention of eventually being overnight stays.

I was excited, but also had very guilty feelings. I was in no way worried about Daisy in someone else's care, after all, she went to nursery and then school. No, I was worried I was giving up on my child, even if it was only for a few hours a week. I was handing her over because I couldn't cope, but I could cope, couldn't I? Was this how social services take your child from you? You read stories like it all the time, my mind was racing.

Miss Trendy, along with this kindly looking lady, walked down my drive. I was spying out of the corner of an upstairs window. Should I answer the door? Daisy made my mind up for me and started head-butting the front door as soon as she heard the bell ring. Thanks, Daisy. I raced downstairs, checked my reflection, yuck, then smiled sweetly and warmly as I invited yet another new stranger into my home.

Daisy immediately launched into a full on attack, so I had to resort to a bribe of Quavers, Milky Buttons and *Teletubbies* on the screen. Peace. The mad woman – sorry, I mean kind, gentle, smiling woman – was like a saint entering my house. I'm sure there was a halo above her head at times (and that's coming from an atheist).

So there we were, Miss Trendy, Mrs Halo and me sitting, smiling. It wasn't long before the conversation was in full flow. I can talk, believe me, usually a load of crap, but I can talk.

Basically, the meeting was to propose Daisy's first stay at Mrs Halo's house. All the forms had been approved and Daisy was to be 'fostered' on a Saturday from nine until four twice a month. Wow, I was elated. Seven whole hours without Daisy and I didn't have to pay! Result!

Likes and dislikes explained, plans made, they left and I felt ok, but glancing over at Daisy sitting on top of the TV table chewing the corner of the flat screen, I couldn't help but feel so sad, so guilty. I was a rubbish mother.

Chapter Twenty-One
The Butterfly

O ne benefit of Daisy being in a special school, was that she could attend their summer play scheme. The scheme is for disabled children and they get one-to-one full-time care provided by trained (I use this term loosely) staff. Daisy could attend for ten days during August and this was a huge bonus. It's not easy for any parent in the summer holidays, but for a parent of a child like Daisy it's hellish. Daisy cannot go to the park to play on the swings, well she could but:

> *She can't sit on a swing.*
> *She can't go down a slide.*
> *She wallops any child within one metre.*
> *She takes food from children's hands.*
> *She kicks ducks!*

The list could go on and on, and suffice to say Daisy cannot go to the park like other children. The same applies to play/activity centres, bowling, swimming, leisure centres, etc.

Anyway, the summer play-scheme was a lifeline. I did worry the first time I left her that the staff didn't fully understand what Daisy was like. They had been given a comprehensive rundown of Daisy and her Daisy-isms, but I still felt uneasy.

Two pretty young girls were assigned Daisy. They had so much enthusiasm I actually felt sorry for them. They bounced with energy and excitement. They were keen, eager, foolish. They clearly didn't appreciate Daisy wasn't like others.

They were fooled by her angelic looks. They tried to take Daisy's hand, she was having none of it, then whoosh, Daisy was off and the two pups followed, shocked. Oh my! Time to go and try to forget what mayhem Daisy could cause in the next couple of hours.

I actually had butterflies in my stomach as I approached the school to collect her that first day. I had repeatedly checked my phone to see if there were any missed calls, but there were none. Perhaps I underestimate Roo? Other parents were bringing their children out proudly looking at art pieces, sculptures made with egg cartons, you know what I mean. Well, in I went and when I announced I was there to collect Daisy, there was a sort of unease amongst the troops.

'Daisy's mum's here,' a girl shouted down the hallway.

'Where's Daisy?' shouted another.

Hmm, I start to wonder what my cherub has been up to. At that I hear a meow. *Here she comes,* I thought. There she was, my sweetheart, like a real bruiser owning the corridor. Two different girls (older, bigger and meaner looking) were trying to keep up with her looking terrified, exhausted, undone. Daisy had no shoes on. Different clothes on than she arrived in. Two dummies in her mouth. A big grin on her chops. She knows she's been bad, I know she knows, she's clever!

Daisy walks straight past me and doesn't even glance at me, I don't exist. This used to make me very upset but you get to accept it. I call her, still no acknowledgment. Then I resort to tactics and offer a biscuit – there, got ya!

I ask how she's been, but don't get an answer. Nothing. I ask why she has different clothes on. Don't get an answer. Oh dear, I don't think it's been a good day. The girls couldn't wait to get Daisy out of the building. I ask them to follow me to the car so they can update me on the first day.

Apparently, one of the first girls assigned to Daisy had been smacked across the back and was so traumatized she'd had to go home sick. The second girl was too scared to look after Daisy and cried for the whole day until being sent home early. Well done, Daisy!

Worried Daisy wouldn't be welcomed back, I strap her in the car and shyly announce I would see them in two days. They grimace and wave us off. Daisy!

Two days later and we were back. As I walked Daisy into the hall, I'm greeted by yet more staff. This time I recognise one of them. She works at Daisy's school and has a bit of experience working with Daisy. Phew, today should be a better day.

She tells me they are going on a trip to see a butterfly farm. *That'll be nice*, I thought, *Daisy likes a good trip out in a minibus. She won't look at a butterfly, but likes a trip nevertheless.*

I waved goodbye to Daisy and felt much happier that it would be a good day.

It was soon time to collect Daisy and there was all sorts of laughter and hysterics going on at the school. As I entered, the staff could not wait to grab me.

'Oh my God, you're not going to believe it,' says an excited girl.

'What, tell me, what's she done now?'

'Jane will tell you, let me get her.'

Bloody hell, I wish they'd hurry up, I think silently.

At that Jane, the supervisor, called me over. 'Annie, there's been a bit of an incident today,' she announced with a slight grin.

'What, is Daisy all right?'

'Yes, Daisy's fine, absolutely fine, never better. Been lovely all day.'

'Go on.'

'Well, Daisy had a great day, sat in her buggy and enjoyed looking at the butterflies, but we made the mistake of going to watch a butterfly demonstration. A butterfly expert was kind enough to allow the children into a netted area and he was talking about all the rare and beautiful butterflies in the enclosure. He held his hand open and a beautiful rare butterfly called a 'bird wing' flew over to him and opened its wings. It was truly glorious.'

Where was this going, I thought in a dread-filled, knowing way.

'Anyhow, we were all admiring the butterfly's beauty, when he announced it was worth five hundred pounds! I don't think he was thinking about his audience when he let it fly around the enclosure, because unfortunately, no, very tragically for the 'bird wing', it landed on Daisy's knee. We knew at that moment tragedy was about to strike, and it did. Daisy scooped the 'bird wing' into her grasp, crumpled it up then tried to eat the remains, but it had literally turned to dust. Gone. Kaput. Finito!'

What could I say to that? My only response was, 'Don't tell me I have to pay five hundred pounds for a bloody butterfly?'

'No, we scampered!' she said embarrassingly. 'We just said our goodbyes, hoping he hadn't noticed, and ran. I don't think we'll be returning any time soon!'

'Poor butterfly,' I said sympathetically. 'Now, let that be a lesson to you, Daisy and any creatures big and small don't mix,' I said through a dry smile.

In a funny sort of way, Daisy endeared herself to the staff that day. I left with an exasperated smile. Oh, Daisy, what am I going to do with you?

Chapter Twenty-Two
Seven

The older Daisy became, the more people would stare. Most of the time I ignored it, but people don't think, they don't care. Yes, Daisy does have to be in a buggy in public. Yes, she does like a dummy to keep her calm, and yes she does make a few strange sounds – as well as her usual meowing, mooing and quacking – but Daisy looks completely normal.

If she had some sort of disfigurement I'm quite sure a lot more people wouldn't openly stare, but because it looks like I have just plonked a bigger than average girl into a buggy and stuffed a dummy in her mouth, Joe public feel the need to judge.

What really bugs me is that when mums, dads, grannies and kids openly gawp and chuckle at Daisy, how do they know she can't understand? How do they know she isn't hurt by the constant pointing and sniggering. It is cruel. I feel so sad for her. I feel so angry at others. Some days if only I had a gun!

I've lost my temper on so many occasions and the anger that sometimes explodes from my tongue can, and often does, cause a scene, but I never have regrets. I may embarrass myself, but I never have regrets. Daisy cannot talk, cannot understand and certainly cannot judge others, therefore, no one has the right to ever judge her. She is just my little girl whose brain doesn't work the way it should.

Daisy has been dealt a very bad card. I'm just so happy she is unaware of it. She is in a very large bubble that provides so much care and love and always will. I will always be there for her, forever.

What saddens me, well all of us, is that she will never have a boyfriend, steal my makeup, drive a car, get married, have a baby, laugh at a joke, enjoy a good film or even argue with us. Why? Because she can't and it's not fair. Her life is not fair. I am so sad for her, for me, for all four of us, for we all suffer in some ways. We all want these things for Daisy and we can't and won't ever witness them.

Chapter Twenty-Three
Dolphins

We work hard, well that's a bit of a lie on my part. Nick works hard and due to his hard work we are fortunate to have a small holiday home in Florida. We go every year and always take Daisy with us. After all, she is a big, big part of our family. Don't get me wrong, it's a bloody nightmare at the airport and on the flight, but the end result is worth the torturous previous hours.

Daisy loves our pool and will happily bite her way through umpteen pairs of armbands, sinking and floating, swallowing and coughing, loving every chlorine filled gulp. I don't much care for the water, so use this as an excuse to be lifeguard (pretend) while the boys have to endure a physical onslaught in the water. Genius!

We have exhausted all the theme parks of Orlando and Daisy is probably on a 'wanted' poster at most. I don't think there is a single character she hasn't bitten. Barney, Dora the Explorer, Mickey, Woody Woodpecker. I could go on.

The embarrassing thing is that Daisy often gets a special viewing with the characters, so it's so awful when she repays the compliment by chewing their felt digits. Barney was by far the worse chomp she ever had. She just wouldn't let go. I could see that at any moment the cover of Barney would be blown and expletives would explode from his mouth, but I came to the rescue and biscuits replaced his purple paw. Phew! I bet he received a 'where there's a blame there's a claim' insurance payout from Islands of Adventure after his meeting with my pet.

Another attraction of Florida is that you can interact with dolphins at Discovery Cove. Having read that dolphins have a special bond with 'special kids' I couldn't wait to experience this and see for myself what bond giant fish and giant girl would have.

I had chosen not to go in the water with Daisy, Nick and Harvey. As previously mentioned, I don't 'do' water and second I bloody detest dolphins. I just don't trust them, it's their human like teeth, wrong! The three of them got kitted out in wet suits (very unflattering for Daisy and Nick) and I sat back in a deck chair, relishing the fact that I would have the next hour in peace and Daisy would be at one with nature.

Into the deep they went, Nick first, then Daisy, followed by Harvey. Daisy wasn't happy. The water was cold. She only liked our pool, which was always at bath temperature. Their assigned dolphin 'Tyler' approached circling them. It was like a scene from Jaws.

Tyler did swim right up to Daisy, but she was having none of it and punched him on the head. Damn, one unhappy dolphin, dolphin trainer and husband. Nick shouted at me to get her out of the water as if it was my fault! There was all sorts of pandemonium going on. Daisy was hitting anyone within fifty centimetres.

Nick was shouting at me, I was screeching back, Harvey wanted the water to swallow him up – just a usual day in our life. So, that was Daisy's 'special bond' with Tyler. Can't say I blame her for clonking him one, after all he had a big sneaky grin on his face and he stunk of fish. Yuck!

Other creatures that Daisy has experienced in Florida have been:

Giant Walrus – she completely ignored it and it was right by her feet in a show at Sea World. All other children (and Nick) had their feet up on their seats screeching. Not Daisy, she just sat and flicked the pages of her book.

Alligator – Daisy escaped from the pool fence and was found by the lake looking at a rather large alligator. Imagine the headlines!

Lizards – many have been rescued from Daisy's imminent appetite.

Raccoons – Nick and Harvey were chased by Ricky the Raccoon, Daisy and myself just strolled past them. Boys are such girls at times.

Jaws – does this count? Daisy was sat on the Jaws ride at Universal Studios, when Jaws leapt out of the water and the whole boat screamed, Daisy just continued to play with a piece of balloon string and didn't flinch.

Daisy does make us laugh.

Chapter Twenty-Four
Nappy Nurse

W hy oh why do so many children with any form of disability seem to be dressed to suit the stereotypical idea that people have? I don't understand it. I have always dressed Daisy beautifully. Believe me, sometimes its not easy getting clothes to fit over her ginormous nappies, but so far to date, I have always managed. I think I do a pretty good job of it, I just have to shop differently.

Clothes have to cover her bum so the nappy doesn't show. Leggings are a saviour, as they suck in her thighs, while tunics cover her lumps and bumps. A-line dresses are a must, she always looks fabulous. School uniforms have to be made as stockists don't supply dresses to cover a nappy bustle. I guess the manufacturers don't think about how a parent dresses a child over the age of five if they are still in a nappy.

Why would they, unless of course they could make a lot of money from it, which they probably can't. There are a few websites of clothing for 'sturdy' kids, but they aren't exactly on trend. However, this digresses from my problem of the way 'special' children are dressed.

Trousers always seem to be far too short, far too tight, mis-matched socks, mis-matched tops, ill-fitting jackets and dull colours. On and on I could go, it's not right. Just because the child doesn't give a hoot how they are dressed doesn't mean they should be dressed as if no one cares. It just re-emphasises people's opinions and degrades these children even more, giving others an excuse to laugh, point and smirk.

Now Daisy has reached the dizzy heights of seven, nappies can no longer be purchased from the supermarket. Daisy has to be assessed to see whether she can have supplies from an incontinence nurse. Bet you never knew that job existed?

The nurse asks a ridiculous amount of questions on Daisy's toilet habits to come up with a reasonable figure to supply per month. After what seems like an age, a figure of three nappies a day is plucked from the air.

Nappy Nurse comes to this conclusion by announcing one is needed for the morning, one for a mid day change and one for the night time. Great, if you have a child that will poo when you are about to do a change or only has a wee three times a day.

Nappy Nurse didn't understand my frustration. Three nappies a day is not adequate. What if she poos, which she will? What if she poos more than once, which she will? What if she wees a lot, which she will?

Then there is the problem of Daisy taking off her nappy if she sees fit. She does like to wave them like a flag. What do I do about that, put it back on even if it is wet? Nappy Nurse, ignoring my last question, just replies that the nappy will hold one and a half litres of water! Fabulous, that's that sorted then!

It takes me months and months to sort out a higher nappy quota. Many hours spent on the telephone, meetings, begging until I finally get four a day. Ah well if they won't give me more, you can get anything on the Internet nowadays. Yes, even giant nappies!

Chapter Twenty-Five
Meeting of the Quacks

An appointment was made for myself, Nick and Daisy to attend a local community hospital to have Daisy assessed by a team of multi-professionals. Nick and I duly attended and know it will be another fruitless waste of time. Assessed for what? We never seemed to know. Nevertheless, you have to attend or you are deemed to be uncooperative.

We are met by an overeager frizzy haired woman. You know the type, no makeup, baggy, creased, far too short trousers. Flimsy tie-died t-shirt stretched over ample sagging breasts and probably my biggest pet hate, flat round-toed, t-bar, clown like shoes – ewh!

Must Be a Vegan, as I have carefully chosen to call her, escorted the three of us into a room, a large room, full of toys and books. She led us in and then said to make ourselves comfortable, as she and her colleagues wouldn't be long.

Tables and chairs circled the room and there was a very large mirror on the end wall. Drawn to the mirror, as any self-respecting woman would be (Must Be a Vegan could have done with a good couple of hours in front of it), I immediately checked out my hair and re-touched my lippy.

Nick was answering a call on his mobile and Daisy, well Daisy, was just circling the room licking anything she could pop into her mouth. After a decent amount of time, Nick started grumbling at me. It's always my fault that they are taking the piss.

I did have to agree, they were taking the piss. Daisy was getting increasingly destructive with each minute that passed and we had by now probably been in the room for a good fifteen minutes. Out came the Quavers, then some custard creams to appease my cherub, then Nick quietly leaned over to me and quipped, 'That's not a fucking mirror.'

'What isn't?' I snapped and then it suddenly dawned on me. They were bloody spying on us. It was a false mirror and they were on the other side watching us – how awful. Not only did I feel utter horror at the fact that we'd been tricked into waiting for a meeting, but also – and this was probably worse – I'd done my lippy and hair in front of them. How embarrassing!

Nick was absolutely furious. He stormed out of the room and was immediately met by Must Be a Vegan, who had clearly realised the game was up. Nick said nothing, just looked like he wanted to kill her. She knew her cover was blown and not to appear unsympathetic, apologised profusely that they had taken so long to join us saying they were now ready.

Not good enough! We were both angry. Daisy by now was trashing the room. *Good,* I thought. We made our excuses to Must Be a Vegan and explained we were very disappointed they'd felt the need to spy on us before they met us. Clearly embarrassed by being caught out, she did try to justify through lots of 'ums' and 'ers' that they were not watching us as parents, but it was purely to identify Daisy and her needs, to get a better understanding of her problems. Yeah, right! They could've just asked.

We were ready to go, pissed off and upset. It was very awkward. Must Be a Vegan was stuttering her words, clearly realising they had over-stepped the mark. Her colleagues joined her and huddled together, almost sitting on each others laps. I had my coat on, Nick had never taken his off, and Daisy was chewing her shoe. I had car keys in my hand, so the signal that we were ready to leave was clear.

'Please, just five more minutes? We won't keep you much longer,' Must Be a Vegan longingly asked. I sat down, too polite for my own good.

'We believe Daisy has Attention Deficit Hyperactivity Disorder and would like her to undergo a set of tests,' announced Must Be a Vegan.

Here we go again, I thought. *Just another guess, another appointment, another waste of everyone's time.*

'What type of tests?' I quizzed, almost being pedantic and insinuating Daisy could hardly fill out a paper.

'Well, an appointment will be made and you'll be asked about things like medical history, any mental health problems, any family history of ADHD, your child's development and temperament. Also, of specific ADHD symptoms, and when they started. Daisy's relationship with you and any other problems Daisy, or you as a parent, may have.'

'Woah, hang on,' I interrupted, 'I think you're barking up the wrong tree. Daisy is active, but she hasn't got a decent enough level of understanding to..." I stopped, speaking. I knew we would have to go along with yet another bloody ridiculous waste of energy appointment.

No one got it, no one got Daisy. Daisy is unique. Typical, I don't just have a special little girl, I have a special little girl who is beyond the understanding of all these know it all's. We would await the next appointment.

Chapter Twenty-Six
The Bath

S o, there I was, lost in a world of peace and tranquility. Relaxed, warm, soaking, dreamy. Daisy sitting on the bathroom floor, licking the edge of the radiator and twiddling the string of her bib. Content, both content.

Ding, dong (again, this is not the real sound of my doorbell). Shit. Ding, dong. Ding, dong. Shit, shit, shit.

I wrapped myself in a towel and rushed down the stairs dripping, unhappy and pissed off. There to greet me was the postman, grinning. I signed for the documents (probably another appointment) and then slammed the door. Excited that my lovely warm bubbly bath awaited, I rushed back upstairs.

Oh my god. Oh My bloody god. I didn't know what to do. There was blood everywhere and I mean everywhere. It was like a scene from Jaws. You know, the bit where he bites the leg off some poor swimmer? Yet again, I digress.

Daisy seemed quite happy. She was sitting on the floor, her back to me. I wondered where the blood was from. I checked my legs as I had just shaved them. No, nothing. No nicks or cuts. Where the hell had all the blood come from? I then nervously looked at Daisy. Oh, Jesus Christ. Her beautiful face was red, her hair was red. Blood soaked her clothes and there in her mouth was the culprit – my razor. No tears from her face, just blood.

She wouldn't let go, she was chewing it like it was a lollipop. Slicing her tongue with each chew and enjoying every single slice that the razor made. I had to physically battle with her to take it from her mouth. She let out an almighty scream, not because she was in any sort of pain, no, she wanted it back. She wanted to chew the bloody razor blade.

I didn't know what to do. Panicking, I remembered Harvey had recently fallen off his bicycle and taken a bite out of the pavement leaving him with his tooth embedded in his lip. That too resulted in a lot of blood and a neighbour of mine brought him home with lots of sugar in his mouth. Apparently this stops the bleeding. I also recalled it actually did. It also takes the injured party's mind off the pain.

I rushed downstairs and grabbed a box of sugar and a spoon. Daisy had stopped protesting when I returned and was sucking the top of a shampoo bottle, leaving it stained a lovely shade of pink. She looked horrendous, like she'd been mauled by a tiger, and a bloody big one at that.

God, why me? I started to spoon the sugar near her mouth. At first, she wasn't having any of it, then she realised it was quite nice. Spoon after spoon soon went in. I could see the lines left by the razor blade across her tongue, probably about eight or ten. Eek, but Daisy didn't seem bothered in the slightest. She was quite happy. No signs of pain, no moaning, nothing! The bleeding did stop, the nightmare was over, marvellous thing sugar.

I sat on my bathroom floor and cried. I cried for a long time. Daisy lay next to me pinching and biting my damp skin. We sat and stared at each other. What next, what on earth could possibly be next?

Chapter Twenty-Seven
The Psychologist (Part Two)

So, here we go again. Some do-gooder who can fix my poor parenting skills, fix my daughter, fix me. A bouncy, bloody over-enthusiastic, excruciatingly annoying know-it-all fresh from reading Pavlov's Dog is the latest house invader. Ivan (she looked like a boy and was a psychologist, the knitted clothes type, so I'm thinking this is a good name, no? Yes, you're right, I'm not all there!) was sizing me up from the off. She was watching my interaction with Daisy, watching, judging.

While Ivan described her planned intentions, Daisy was getting restless. Pushing, grabbing, pinching. I tried to ignore but I couldn't win.

'By ignoring Daisy, you're not encouraging development,' spat Ivan.

I said nothing. I was furious, but said nothing. Daisy continued bombarding me with her affectionate pinches, so I thought I'd show Ivan how real parents rock. I pinched Daisy sharply on her arm and then pushed her onto the sofa! Jeez, what was I thinking? Ivan was horrified. She jostled with her note pad in shock at what I'd just done in front of her.

Daisy on the other hand was loving it, wanting more and more pushes from me, pinching me harder. Oh no, why didn't I wait until Ivan had left?

'Annie, you really shouldn't do that, I strongly advise you don't do that again. I am going to have to tell my supervisor.'

'Shit, sorry. So sorry. She likes rough play.' My words meant nothing, but did I really care? Take her from me, no one will keep her, just take her!

Loving the 'rough' play, Daisy decided to engage with Ivan. Threateningly closing in on her, she squared up and then swiped the unsuspecting target's glasses, causing them to perch neatly between eye and chin. Ivan dropped her guard, yet another professional to do so.

Red, with a mix of embarrassment and anger, Ivan took Daisy's hand and in an unconvincing 'gentle' grapple, led her from the room shutting the door firmly behind her.

'Daisy will now seek approval that we are not mad with her. She will try and enter the room, but Mum, you must be firm and keep leading her out of the room and closing the door. Eventually, she will display some degree of upset and this will show she has a level of understanding of right and wrong,' Ivan enthused and continued. 'Mum, you must be firm with her, but loving at the same time...'

Blah, blah, blah. On and on she went, trying to educate me about my petal who didn't salivate when entering a room like the Pavlov dogs she had so tirelessly studied. Who didn't follow the basics of human cognitive disciplines, but just broke all the rules, every single one of them.

Three minutes was the first milestone to wait while Ivan held the door handle tight. We waited – not a peep. We waited, and waited. I knew Daisy wouldn't be whimpering behind the door, but Ivan assured me she would be.

Five minutes was reached it was becoming uncomfortable

and, in my humble opinion, unsafe to leave Daisy unsupervised. Ivan with an air of excitement threw open the door expecting a sad, subservient Daisy to be sat with her head in her hands waiting for approval and praise – not Daisy!

Daisy was nowhere to be seen. I ran to the kitchen and she was sat on the floor of the kitchen, nappy to the side of her, eating a banana with the skin on. Snatching it out of her mouth I was angry. Not with Daisy, with Ivan. Daisy doesn't 'do' what the textbooks say children will do. When would people listen to me? She is not from a usual mould!

Ivan seemed uncomfortable but left with a wry smile on her face. I shut the door and wondered what response would come from this meeting. Had I been foolish pushing Daisy? Daisy always loved being pushed but was it right to do it? Of course it was.

Chapter Twenty-Eight
New Car

It was time to purchase a new car. Daisy was getting too big. Well, that was my excuse to have a nice new 4x4. Now that she needed a wheelchair to ferry her around in public, I needed a bigger boot. We went to a garage not too far away and got immersed in the whole sales pitch and excitement of shiny vehicles. We really are shit parents at times. Forgetting we weren't your usual family suddenly hit us hard when a guy came running into the showroom asking if anyone was missing a little girl. My heart sank, fear enveloped me.

Oh My God, where is Daisy?

I thought Nick had her, he thought I had her.

The man explained, in a panicked state, that Daisy had just walked in front of his car on the dual carriageway. Luckily for her, he'd seen her well in advance thanks to her bright pink and lemon dress and very long hair. Yep, she'd walked out of the garage, across a road – completely ignoring the fact that cars were a bit scary – and then walked into a muddy field on her way to goodness knows where. What were we doing all this time? Looking at coloured bits of plastic deciding what would look nicest on the drive.

I would have given Usain Bolt a run for his money, as I have never moved so fast in my life. I was running and calling her name, so she decided to run as well, but away from me! It seemed like an eternity until I caught up with her, all sorts of horrendous thoughts rushing through my mind. Daisy just had no concept of fear or danger.

Yet again, Daisy made me cry.

Chapter Twenty-Nine
Eight

We have all heard of Time Out, yes? I never had a problem with locking Harvey in the chiller (or conservatory as it is known to normal families), he could be a cheeky little bleeper when it suited so some time to reflect on his actions never hurt him. However, finding out from my special secret source at school (she knows who she is) that a 'Time Out' room was being used for Daisy, well that opened up a mahoosive can of ginormous worms.

It was fortuitous timing that a parents evening was imminent so rather than contact the school with my inside information I decided to bide my time and question the school in a calm (cough), sensible (double cough), appropriate platform. The day of reckoning came. Team Rainey arrived at the school and waited to be called to hear all about Daisy's progress (sniggers) and hit the teacher (not literally, though it had crossed my mind many times) with the 'Time Out' bombshell.

Now, if I were a school that didn't have stringent procedures in place, didn't have policies covering my ass for any eventuality and hid child management practices from parents, would I put a sign on a room that wasn't covered by any such policy or procedure for all to see? Guess that would be a dumb thing to do, yes, no?

We were called to the classroom with a smile. We walked past a door emblazoned with 'Time Out Room', we are slightly stunned, its true! I give the teacher who I am choosing to offer you no description as I will end up in a court room, a gritted smile. I had decided I would wait to listen to the usual bullshit but then Harvey blurted out:

'Mum, when are you going to ask about 'Time Out?'

A crimson teacher faced us. I too felt a little warm. Here goes... So, a discussion was had, heated, fraught, angry. A denial of such a room existing, of being used. Lies upon lies.

'But, how do you explain the sign on the door down the corridor?' we questioned.

'There is no such room,' teacher with no description angrily blurted.

Out we stomped like petulant children and point proudly with a 'ta da' at the sign and then, as if to beggar belief, the sign is torn from the door.

'There is NO TIME OUT ROOM,' teacher with no description screams.

We smile, this is not the end.

Lets skip a week. A meeting was scheduled. Head teacher (a joke), Deputy Head (an absolute tit), Teacher (a *^*^) some jobsworth from the councils education department (bigger *^*^ than the teacher), Nick (stay off your phone and pay attention) and little old me. The odds were stacked against me, with only Nick on my side but I've grown a big pair of balls over the years, have had to.

I listed my concerns, my disappointment, my worries, my

anxiety. I explained that Daisy's management should never be by means of locking her in a room, alone, empty, self-harming out of frustration. I cried, angry tears. I asked to see the school's policy on 'Time Out'. I noticed shuffling of papers. Yep, they didn't have one. I asked to see the supposed parent consent I had signed (according to the tit), couldn't be found. I asked why they thought it appropriate to lock Daisy in a room. I asked why she was strapped in a buggy in the classroom (restraint) – cheers spy! I asked many probing questions. Each question was answered with either raised eyebrows, rolling of eyes, rude, abrupt big words from the *^*^ from the council. One reply floored me though.

'Mrs Rainey, I have a lot more knowledge about the brain than you do, Daisy was in crisis and therefore needed to be put in isolation,' Deputy Tit proclaimed.

'So locking her in a room, that apparently doesn't exist, so she can hit herself and multiply her distress is the correct course of action for Daisy?' I asked.

'Mrs Rainey, I think I know your child better than you do,' Tit smirked.

Wow, just wow!

I walked out. This was just one of countless meetings at the school, each churning up failures in their procedures. Each highlighting untruths. Each making me very unpopular with the school and the council, but each very necessary to make Daisy's voice heard. Things got worse before they got better, a lot worse, I still have the photos of unexplained incidences that caused horrific bruising to Daisy in school. No actions were ever taken despite endless complaints. Shameful. Exhausting.

The school eventually had a management review, a new head teacher and things got better. Deputy Tit remained but we kept a wide berth, he knew not to catch my eye but I made it very clear to all that as Daisy had no voice, I would always be hers and nothing would pass me that wasn't right, however unpopular I was made to feel.

Chapter Thirty
Behaviours

Daisy's idiosyncratic behaviours had started to get weirder. Her latest pleasure came from eating the front of her footwear, yes you've read correctly, she ate shoes! There had been many little whims over the years, the head butting obvs, the hair twiddling then swallowing causing actual fur balls (WTF), the hair twiddling and then tugging from scalp causing bloody big bald patches (A consultant who shall remain nameless but she knows who she is − FG, helpfully advised shaving Daisy's hair off through this episode- thanks, great advice but we'll pass), biting her nails completely off leaving open wounds, the list goes on and on and on but her latest you couldn't even make up.

She would sit quite content, foot adorned with shoe in mouth (very flexible due to hyper mobility), chomping through the leather. Only I could have a child that did this, surely? No shoe was safe and all ended their short life with an open toe. Why not just buy sandals, I hear you cry. We did, and she'd just move further up until sourcing the leather).

Forget the obvious hygiene issues, Daisy's footwear fetish was costing me a small fortune. The behaviour lasted a good six months only to be followed by nose punching, which sadly remains the case even today. Her nose has been broken so many times its not possible to give a figure. She bashes it when happy, she bashes it when sad. All I can do is distract, but its alarming and upsetting and awful and makes everyone around wince. Why does she do these things. Who knows? Nobody.

Chapter Thirty-One
Nine

I had just finished work and had pulled onto the driveway at home. Sitting in the car, engine off, I checked my phone.

I saw the notifications. Five missed calls from an unknown caller and one voice message. I listened, the tone was serious:

'Mrs Rainey, this is social services, could you please (not sure they said please) arrange to bring Daisy to the children's centre at the Royal Gwent Hospital straight away? You will be met by a member of our team and we will explain when you get there.'

Phone goes dead.

I sat wondering, anxiety rushing through me like a bullet train. What was I going to be greeted with when entering the house. In I tentatively crept. 'Everything OK?' I asked.

'Yes, she's a happy girl, full of cheek,' was the response from her after school carer.

I looked at Daisy, nothing had changed, her head wasn't caved in, her limbs seemed intact, all seemed pretty normal.

'I have to take her to hospital straight away,' I explained.

'Why?' came a concerned voice.

'No idea,' was my response.

Changing her nappy, stuffing my bag with crisps, biscuits, Fimbles, picture books, we were ready. I strapped Daisy into the car and off we drove.

We arrived, although parking was a bloody nightmare, but hey thank God I had a Blue Badge. Getting out of the car and ignoring the stares from the ignorant queuing fleet, I strapped madam into her HUGE buggy. In we trotted by now my heart was pumping so fast I felt I may soon need a hospital bed all to myself.

A stern looking woman seemed to be waiting for us.

'Hi, are you Daisy?' she asks an uninterested face who's only interest is trying to get out of her strap.

'She can't talk,' I explain.

'I know,' came a really bloody bitchy reply.

I could feel my horns creaking out of my skull. *Stay calm*, I thought.

'Have you been told why you are here?' was the next question from Bitch woman.

'Sorry, I don't know, is it to do with test results?' came my innocent reply.

'Come into this room,' was the response.

In we went, by now Daisy was almost choking on her buggy strap, I had to let her out or she would croak it and that would be a bit awkward. This was a big mistake, as it was like letting the air out a balloon and watching it bounce off all the walls. Crisps came out, calm was restored.

'Daisy has bruising on her inner thighs,' Bitch exclaimed in a low tone, 'can you tell us how they got there, Mrs Rainey?' Instantly insinuating *I* was guilty of abuse.

Dismissively I replied, 'Oh, she's always got bruises from something or other, let me see.'

'We have contacted the police. They are on their way.

We will need to take photos. Is that OK?'

Whoa! My head started to spin, 'The police? Why?'

What happened next was so upsetting. My poor girl was undressed (reluctantly and swiping at the Bitch – good!), photographed from every angle (giving the photographer a healthy kick in the process) and it was only when Daisy had peed on the floor – I wish she had dumped – that I was allowed to put a nappy on her and dress her. It was so cold, bless her, but thankfully she was so oblivious to all that was going on that she was completely unaffected – me, however, that's a different story.

The questioning began all while I was trying to stop Daisy from escaping the room. It was a blur. All eyes were on me like I was some sort of monster. I felt guilty, looked guilty, but was not guilty.

It turns out, a member of staff from her summer play scheme had concerns about two bruises on Daisy's inner thigh, and thought she may have been pinned down (I am guessing they thought in a sexual way, but that's either because I am sick in the head or that's the world we live in today), anyhow, instead of calling me and asking if I had noticed them or could explain, she rightly, or wrongly, called social services and reported me. Now don't get me wrong, I get that there are some evil people in this world and this sort of thing sadly for many does go on, but if they knew me, my family and how we manage Daisy, there should never have been any questions raised, and also, Daisy's as strong as an ox. Good luck to anyone abusing her sexually or physically, you'd get battered!

I felt I was guilty. I felt I looked I was guilty. I felt I was about to internally combust, my neck sweating. I was condemned and felt I had to quantify how good a parent I was. I knew they thought I was abusing her and I had to stay calm. So why, WHY, did I think it was a good idea to be defensive?

'Do you really think I could abuse Daisy even if I wanted to?' Why would I even say that?

I could see eyebrows raise, darting eyes around the room, I was digging a big hole and they were handing me the shovel.

'Good luck finding someone to look after Daisy!' My mouth was now in a dangerous conversation, shut up, Annie.

Awkwardness is abundant, tension at boiling point.

Daisy by now was in meltdown and I was trying to ignore her yelps and moans but she did me a favour, they have had enough of her, you can tell, she'd pinched, head butted, tipped chairs, licked every surface, shoe, floor tile. She'd had enough. They had had enough of her. They let me leave. I wasn't arrested. I was allowed to keep her. I had to await their report. They must have trusted me (now there's a first).

So, the outcome. It was accepted that my explanation – that I had more than likely held her too tight when changing her nappy, which believe me is like putting a nappy on an escaping snake, was accepted. You're all wondering, ooh, could it be the father? (Sick lot), the answer, absolutely not, do you think he ever changes her nappy? Ha!

Chapter Thirty-Two
Ten

Lucifer is sitting in Hell. He's got a long checklist:

'Lets give her a beautiful girl, but lets give it a twist.' Tick.

'Let the intensive crying begin.' Tick.

'Lets throw in no sleep.' Tick.

'Is that bloody woman still going? Right, lets up the game! Add epilepsy, that'll do it.' Tick.

'Just for safe measure, pop in some idiosyncrasies to screw with her.' Tick.

'She still going, still married? FFS! OK, lets give the child an appetite, make her chunky.' Tick.

'Oh, and aggressive and agitated inexplicable behaviours.' Tick.

'Still going? Still not in jail? Still not driven off a cliff?Right, I've had enough... WARTS, give the child warts.'

You couldn't make it up. Daisy started getting the odd wart on her fingers, which initially didn't cause me to react. I purchased the usual treatments and stupidly thought they would disappear over time. How wrong. Daisy couldn't just get one or two warts on her tiny perfect fingers, no, every digit became horridly saturated, no spare clear skin to be seen. But it didn't stop on her fingers, of course it didn't. Backs of hands were followed by a spectacular leap to (drum roll)

HER FACE!

Her dribbly lips were now just mounds of ugly, lumpy hideousness; her nose was closing in as warts were surfacing the entrance and hanging like grapes; her eyelids didn't escape either, day by day a new one appeared, uglier and more awful than the last.

None of it bothered Daisy, she was, as always, oblivious. But me, it really affected me. I could cope with seizures, I could cope with just a few hours sleep, I could cope with everything she had thrown at me so far, but warts! Nah! Not playing.

Something had to be done.

The GP didn't care. 'Least of her problems,' was the resounding response, 'they will run their course.'

What the GPs didn't quite 'get' though was how it was affecting me. I had this girl that had turned my life upside down, some would say, and I would agree, ruined my life (off to meet Lucifer I go), who was challenging my sanity every single day and the only thing I could cling to was her cuteness. That had now gone, she looked horrible and I really struggled and I know most reading will think what a fucking awful mother, but I just wanted what everyone else had and I couldn't have it and I guess the warts were just a huge test of my strength (or obvious lack of it).

I arranged to see Mr Nice, he would help, yes he was a neurologist but he was also everything to me and Daisy, he would definitely help. He did. He arranged for us to see a dermatologist and within a very few weeks we did. The dermatologist was great and sympathetic and understanding, everything you want when you present like some nutty superficial mother. She agreed to remove the warts at Daisy's next anaesthetic procedure, which coincidently was imminent. At last, someone listened, cared.

While at the appointment with Mr Nice – the one where he referred us to the dermatologist, he took the opportunity to try a new medication on Daisy for her epilepsy, this was a regular 'experimental' activity but I suppose if you don't try you'll just never know what will work.

Anyhow, the medication was called lacosamide and I thought we'd give it a go. It was added to her other medications in my usual crushing/mixing kitchen laboratory and in her chops it went, twice a day, under duress. Four days later, bad, **BAD**, seizures. Long, worrying, endless, blue lips, eye rolling, body jerking fits. I blamed the new drug, I weened her off.

About a week passed and Daisy slowly recovered from the nasty evil seizures and we noticed a very odd side effect. The warts were literally disappearing in front of our very eyes. Over maybe just three days, they were gone, literally all gone. If I believed in a higher being then I would have thought this was a miracle, but I truly do believe it was the lacosamide.

When I informed the doctors about said miracle, they didn't really remark, you would have thought they would have at least documented the remarkable anti-wart properties of the drug, but nothing. They weren't interested. I didn't pursue the potential multimillion pound discovery I had stumbled across, I was just ecstatic that Daisy no longer resembled a toad. I think the docs were just grateful that she would take up less of their time, I was grateful for her flawless skin, for once a medication she had taken, albeit briefly, had done good.

Chapter Thirty-Three
The Seaside

I don't like the beach, well I would if it was a desert island with no kids and an open bar but on the whole I don't like the beach. As a parent you have to do the beach 'thing' though don't you? Making sandcastles, burying Dad in a hole, paddling on the shore.

We were in Clearwater, Florida. It was hot. Daisy and Harvey could barely move their limbs due to the amount of high factor thick suntan lotion I had smothered them in. Why we thought it a good day to go to the beach who knows, but we did. Paying an extortionate sum for the hire of two loungers and an umbrella we settled down for the day.

Harvey *had* to have some sort of floatation device to take into the sea so he obviously chose a lobster the size of a small family car. Off he ran, excited, with strict instructions to stay within waving distance of us. Yes, I know, shit parenting right there. Nick settled down thinking he could have a snooze. Oh no, Mr, you are on Harvey duty, I don't 'do' water. I will take care of devil child.

I am still to this day, angry that I chose to look after Daisy that day, for no sooner had I said, 'I will look after Daisy,' whoosh, off she had scarpered. Arghhhhhhh!

*

First stop, the deck chair of an unsuspecting Mexican family. Plonk, she sat right in the middle of their family group. It felt like an age. They were speaking at a rapid speed to each other, arms waving, while I stood there trying to explain by saying in a very loud slow voice, 'SORRY, SHE DOESN'T UNDERSTAND. SORRY, SORRY.'

It was an age, I'm guessing twenty minutes of pure agony. Twenty minutes of stares, gesticulating, incredulous looks.

Suddenly, madam had had enough. Up she got, walking right through the family group's 'space' with her sandy feet soiling their clean blankets only to PLONK down on a towel next to some food that one of the older Mexicans was setting out. Oh my giddy aunt. I wanted the world to stop spinning. They all gathered round, stern looks etching into my crimson face and then I saw the most wonderful sight, a huge green lobster calling Daisy's name.

'Daisy, Roosty Bear, come on! Yum Yum,' shouted the lobster. Up she got, clapping, smiling, but not without leaning on a plate of some god awful looking food that even she didn't feel the need to steal, contaminating it with her sandy paws en route to the lobster. I wanted to kiss it. I wanted to cry.

Daisy, the lobster and me returned to our area of beach, my head down, feeling the whole of Clearwater were staring, it was then that I nearly committed murder. I could hear him from ten feet away. Nick, sprawled on the sun lounger, snoring, dribbling, burning. Oh how I wanted to let him burn to the point of needing skin grafts. How dare he fall asleep!

I did an awful thing. I told Harvey to go and sit up on the rocks with his green friend. I then, startled my devoted husband.

'Where's Harvey, where's Harvey?' I panicky shrieked.

Nick bolted up. 'What? Errr, where, errr.'

'He's gone,' I cried.

Nick ran down to the shoreline, running into the water, calling in a frantic manner, searching, pacing... I sat and waited. Waiting for him to return, waiting to hear what he would say. He returned with panic enveloping him.

'What are you doing,' he screamed. 'Call the bloody police!'

I sat, eyes eating through him, I pointed to the rocks. He knew what I had done, he knew it was a cruel lie, but he also knew he couldn't argue.

Our lovely family day at the beach ended. Poor Harvey had another day cut short because we just couldn't have a normal day out. Not speaking, we packed up our paraphernalia, changed into day clothes, the lobster got deflated and off we stomped to the car. Then, just when we thought things couldn't possibly get any more dire, Daisy did a runner, like Forrest Gump!

Run, run, run, straight into the sea. She kept on going, deeper, deeper, Nick was untying his laces as she was at waist level, never any urgency with him, she kept on walking. I was screaming for him to get her, he caught up with her at about chin level. I was hyperventilating. Soaked through they both exited the water. I just sat on the sand, Harvey held my hand. We smiled to each other.

Chapter Thirty-Four

Eleven

Nick was now working in Sierra Leone, you couldn't make that up could you? Six weeks away, two weeks home, nothing more to add really just that we seemed to get along much better, absence makes the heart, and all that.

Nick and I landed in Tampa, Florida. My phone went into overdrive as soon as I had signal So, while the cases were being thrown across the conveyor belt, I listened to my many answer phone messages. My heart sank.

It was Daisy's eleventh birthday the day we flew out. What bloody awful parents. Who leaves their child to go on holiday? In my pretty shabby defence, she hadn't a clue it was her special day. Happy Birthday is a song sung most days. I lie, it's sung every day. Anyhow, digressing again, I listened to my messages.

What are the odds of your child (slim if it's a boy, I guess) starting their very first period on firstly their eleventh birthday and secondly, when you're not even in the country.

Yep, Daisy had hit the jackpot, three seizures and her first period all in the space of ten hours, bloody great. I spent the next week not enjoying myself, calling constantly, feeling so guilty, so anxious, so sad. I also felt an enormous pressure to smile for my husband, to try to look nice, he gave me everything I wanted, but all I gave him was sadness. I couldn't win.

Our trip ended, reality returned but I was now on a new controversial, conversation killing mission, some (well probably most) would say a dangerous road to go down. I had long thought of what I would do when Daisy's periods began, had done a little research, but not knowing if she would ever have them hadn't actually gone that step further, until now.

What was the point of Daisy having periods? Daisy would never have sex (or a boyfriend for that matter), she would never have a baby unless, lets be frank, she was raped and even then she couldn't carry a baby to term. Her periods didn't need to continue and I would help her.

I arranged, via Mr Nice, for Daisy to see a gynaecologist who just so happened to be the drop dead gorgeous gynaecologist who delivered Daisy. Mr 'Yes I Would' was a dream of a guy. He listened as I went on and on about the reasons why I wanted to request Daisy be accepted for a hysterectomy, yes, a hysterectomy. Why shouldn't she? It was surely, in the long-term, the absolute best decision for her. Imagine, no more periods, equating to less seizures – as Daisy was now also having what are called Catamenial seizures, which relate to hormonal levels in the body – less pain, less discomfort and lets face it, less smell and unpleasantness for the person changing her nappy. I expected him to dismiss everything but no, he actually agreed, he bloody agreed. Mr 'Yes I Would' told me he would speak to a few colleagues, but as far as he was concerned he was happy to do the surgery and agreed it was in Daisy's best interest.

*

Months passed, many months and a follow up appointment was arranged. This time Mr 'YIW' was wearing scrubs, oh my! The appointment sadly did end very disappointingly though. Mr 'YIW' had done quite a bit of research and explained that he didn't think it would be possible for him to carry out the procedure any time soon. Apparently no child in the UK had EVER had a hysterectomy for non-medical (which this would be classed as) reasons. A case in America which was very similar ended with the mother and doctor going to prison. Also, a disabled person's advocate had reacted horrifyingly to the suggestion of my plans in an ethics forum and explained she would take my case to the Court of Human Rights if I tried to proceed as unbelievably, she bleated that Daisy had the right to have a child, yeah, OK, love!

'This could get messy,' he said with a sigh (oooh, he sighed, so lovely).

I shall not give up. Still to this day I believe it would be in her best interests, but as it stands, she is still 'with womb' for now!

Chapter Thirty-Five
That School Bench

There have been too many 'incidents' in school to write about and I know I can be a little over-anxious when it comes to Daisy being cared for, but when your child cannot tell you about their day, or even give an indication as to whether they have had a good or bad one, you have to be vigilant and pick up on the signs. No need to be Miss Marple on this occasion though, the evidence was imprinted deep into Daisy's body.

Luckily for me, I had a great spy who worked at the school. I had received a call saying that there had been an incident in Daisy's class and she had heard from a reliable source that a member of staff had kicked a pupil, she didn't say which pupil or which staff member, but was giving me the heads up. The trouble with knowing this information was that I could never act on it for fear of my spy losing their job.

It was five o'clock and as usual I had pre-filled the bath, waited an age for Daisy to venture into the bathroom and got to work undressing, un-hair-tying, nappy tearing, just a normal everyday procedure. As my little lump of loveliness lay down enjoying the Jacuzzi bubbles something caught my eye. At first I thought it was her hair shadowing her body, but as I took a closer look I was horrified. Daisy had the biggest, darkest, most awful bruise I had ever seen. It looked a bit like an iron mark, it panicked me. My god it must have hurt, my poor girl. I quickly bathed her; hair, face, pits, foof, bum, waited another age for her to decide to get out and then started to take photos – many, many photos. I couldn't actually believe what I was seeing. Surely Daisy wasn't the pupil who had been kicked? Surely that wasn't a shoe print? I decided that I had to call social services and seek advice as I didn't want a repeat of the 'abuse' photo shoot the previous year.

Explaining the bruise to the social worker, but not my thoughts as to how it got there, she said I would have to contact the school. She probably thought I was over-exaggerating as she hadn't seem too bothered. Thinking about it I probably did sound like a right nutter on the phone. I didn't sleep that night; I kept mulling over and over who could possibly have done this and why no one contacted me when she surely must have been in a lot of discomfort. I called the school first thing, demanding to speak to the head, and an appointment was made.

Now you would think that if a parent complained about such an awful mark on their child the school would be apologetic, remorseful, but not this school. The head was so dismissive insisting absolutely nothing had happened to Daisy at school that day, she had checked the incident book and nothing was noted. I asked for Daisy to be brought to the office. On seeing the bruise you could see the colour drain from the head's face. This was not a normal looking bruise, it was bad, and the type you could be arrested for. She called my old friend Deputy Tit to take a look. He couldn't bear to be in the same room as me, but had to be professional and on seeing the bruise said an investigation would be carried out. I knew by their faces and reactions that they knew what caused the bruise. They were covering up their school's complete inadequacies. I would be contacted later that day.

How strange then that a couple of hours later I got a call from the head. She was chirpy, upbeat and pretending to be my best friend. She explained she had asked Daisy's class teacher if there had been any incidents they could recall from the day before where Daisy would have been upset.

Apparently, they suddenly remembered she had fallen onto a bench in the school yard, cried for a very short time and it was written in the school incident book. The head explained she had looked in the 'wrong' book, unbelievable but also so frustrating for me as I knew what had caused it but could do nothing about it. I believe they knew I knew, the class staff knew I knew. My poor girl. I guess the only good thing to come from this incident was that nothing passed me by, nothing. I questioned everything, every mark, every scratch, I wanted an explanation for everything. I couldn't and can't protect Daisy every hour of the day but I can look out for her and be her voice, and believe me, I have a gob on me.

Chapter Thirty-Six

Twelve

Nick was always desperate to go to Florida, me not so. It was such an ordeal at the airport, on the plane, at border control, but when Daisy was twelve Nick decided it would be nice to have Christmas Day in the villa. We flew out on Christmas Eve, Nick and I took it in turns to babysit Daisy on the flight.

Nick always had her on take off and landing, and I always fed her, we would then take it in turns to patrol the plane with Daisy leading the way, up and down the aisles, for hours, crikey, we must have been the family no one wanted to be on a plane with. If she wasn't getting her twenty thousand steps in, she was kicking the seat in front or trying to grab the occupants of neighbouring seats, it was always a very trying nine hours probably for the passengers just as much as us.

She has injured air hostesses, hit passengers, screamed like she's been stabbed, moo'd, meowed, barked, just a joyful experience. Then, just to top it off on this blissful flight, and might I add, on Nick's watch, Daisy decided to have a nice bowel evacuation. Yep, up the back job. The seat was covered, her clothes and hair were covered and I had to get her to the back of the plane while people were covering their faces with anything they could find. That experience, right there was hell. Harvey hid under a blanket, he wanted a gun. Of course, you can't just take Daisy in a plane toilet, two of you don't fit, nope, I had to get the air steward to curtain off the back of the plane, lie Daisy on the floor, clean her with a pack of baby wipes, deodorise her with something the air steward gave me (smelt like old lady) and then wrap her in a Virgin red blanket to take the walk of shame back to her shit smelling seat that was now covered in a contamination cover sheet. Eyes were stabbing me but what could I do but smile while screaming inside. We landed, we waited for Daisy's wheelchair and for the crowds of stares to leave. It was over and we had arrived.

Our first stop was Publix (an American version of Waitrose), as we knew we had to buy some sort of Christmas dinner fodder. We got there twenty minutes before closing, phew! We bought a poxy runt of a chicken (no turkeys, that's a Thanksgiving thing) some veg (no parsnips or sprouts much to Harvey's delight), a load of junk food and a trolley load of wine. Sorted, well I was at least.

We arrived at the villa and hadn't even noticed that Daisy seemed a bit quiet. Then we smelt that knowing smell, vomit. Jeez, what else, FFS. She was covered in it, it was exiting her mouth in rhythmical moves as Harvey and Nick both feigned nausea squealing like girls. She was fitting, just great, just bloody great.

That night she had to have rescue medication (which I never tend to use as I don't like the side effects), she had about fourteen seizures, every hour, each one I thought she would die, she went so blue. I lay with her all night, holding her but also feeling such guilt for spoiling the boys Christmas Eve.

We had just had the worst twenty-four hours and it was so sad. Nick and Harvey put up a Christmas Tree we had arranged to be delivered. We just wanted to be like everyone else, and went through the motions.

Christmas Day was surreal. Daisy was post ictal (after seizure sleep state) it was twenty-seven degrees, Santa had promised Harvey a new iMac (so he was happy), Nick was happy with his headphones in, cleaning the pool, and me, I was just sat holding Daisy's hand, holding, staring, wondering why us. Lunch, it was shit! Christmas dinner needs sprouts and turkey.

It was six days before Daisy recovered. Six days of worry – days four and five she seemed to loose her sight, she just couldn't focus or seem to see anything, but we were just assuming, we don't know, couldn't ask her. Six days of me sat, eating sour cream and chive Lays crisps (wow, just wow) and litre bottles of wine. As luck may have it, a friend of Harvey's from school happened to be in the same area of Florida, and had agreed to take Harvey to the theme parks with them, thank goodness. Of course, Harvey wanted me (not Nick as he's a pussy and won't go on the rides) to go with him, but I couldn't. He understood but it didn't ease my guilt. Harvey always did have a pretty rough deal, poor kid but such a kind boy.

The only benefit of Daisy's illness (always look for positives) was that following her post ictal state she was lethargic and in a can't-be-arsed-to-move state so this was a massive relief for our many post Christmas shopping trips. We could actually shop and she didn't attempt to take racks of clothes down or scream and create havoc whenever crossing a shop threshold.

The holiday came to an end and we returned home and were very lucky to be upgraded to first class – there must be a God. Thankfully, Daisy slept (well, was drugged) all the way home. I drank, Nick watched many movies and Harvey played games. We were on our way home and we were all good.

Chapter Thirty-Seven
Thirteen - The Hospice

Daisy has been going to a hospice for respite since the age of about eleven. When we were first approached by the hospice (Ty Hafan in Sully, South Wales) both Nick and I were in two minds. We were worried that Daisy would be disruptive to life-limited children, but we were also worried that we would be upset seeing those children. But, Daisy was classed as life-limited with an expectancy of nineteen years – where that number was plucked from, God knows, but that is the age her life is expected to extinguish.

The first time we took Daisy was filled with massive trepidation. We took her as a family and arranged to stay in one of their family rooms for the weekend so that we could be on hand to give advice regarding looking after madam, but also to be there in case she caused mayhem. We packed as if we were going away for a month. Nick and I were both extremely anxious that the hospice would be a sad place, we dreaded the visit.

We arrived, and let's cut to the chase, Daisy had the most amazing weekend. The staff were incredible. The hospice was the happiest of homes from home. Daisy had all the attention she craved, wrapping all the fabulously caring staff around her little finger. We held back, stayed in the background and felt relief. Ty Hafan was a huge help to us and the most incredibly joyful experience for Daisy.

Ty Hafan became our two weeks a year respite, which Nick and I both loved and Daisy also had a much needed break from me!

As far as getting a break from caring twenty-four seven for Daisy, I guess I have been lucky. Daisy had quite a package of support largely due to me constantly pestering/ nagging/ being a humongous pain in the arse to the disabled children's team that I think I wore them down; but also they had admitted that if I were unable to care for Daisy, they had nowhere to place her, even Lovely Lady couldn't cope with her anymore and she was an expert!

Daisy spent four nights a month at a respite home for disabled children. I never felt comfortable leaving her, and every night she stayed I would spend an evening filled with anxiety, so I'm not sure the respite did me much good. There were always queries regarding medication, seizures, behaviours – the list goes on. Daisy also had carers take her out on a Sunday morning for a couple of hours. This was hit and miss with staff. Some were amazing, some were not. Again, my anxiety levels questioned whether it was worth it.

The other help I got was two afternoons and a Saturday morning where two carers would look after Daisy from school and take her out for a nice walk or drive on a Saturday. Once again, hit and miss with staff, but on the whole most were amazing. I did have my fair share of useless ones too.

When you have to hand over your child to the care of others it is not easy, especially when that child is so trusting and cannot communicate. On the one hand you are desperate for the break, really desperate. On the other you don't trust anyone. Can anyone really love looking after another person's child especially when that child can be horrible, hurt you, ignore you? I guess the answer must be yes, but as a mum it's always been such a struggle, something I am still finding hard to do and something that will always haunt me.

Where's the bottle, I need a drink!

Chapter Thirty-Eight
Fourteen

The care and support surrounding special needs children and adults has moved beyond recognition even in the last thirty years. As a child I don't remember seeing children like Daisy in public. Where were they? Sadly, and I'm no expert, I believe they were in institutions of some sort, taken away from their families early on in their lives, placed in homes that treated them more like inmates. I may be wrong but there is no other explanation.

Daisys were not seen when I was young. This is both heart breaking and so wrong, and it's hard to understand that cruelty and ill-treatment of kids like Daisy could ever happen, but it did, does and probably always will. This leads me nicely onto Osceaola State Fair.

Chapter Thirty-Nine
All the Fun of the Fair

As we drove around the roads of Florida for a change, 'cos that's how we rock, we stumbled upon a rather large sign pointing to a rather large field. 'OSCEOLA STATE FAIR'. We drove closer, thinking it looked a bit 'red-neck' but it was a nice day. We hadn't any other plans so thought, let's go see what Harvey can spend our money on!

As we got to the car park there were quite a few protestors with placards – vegan-type, knitted clothes, dreadlocks – you get the picture. We ignored this. We didn't even check out the signs (error) and parked up. I must admit that we seemed a bit out of place. We looked too picture perfect, too clean, too normal (never thought I'd say we looked normal), too many white teeth!

The first thing we saw was a cage, a big cage. To be able to see what was in this cage you had to climb up quite a hill of steps, so as I had Daisy in her wheelchair, Nick and Harvey took the trip. They returned quite quickly insisting I wouldn't want to see what they'd just witnessed, so obviously I gave Nick Daisy's wheelchair and off I stomped, Harvey in tow. Jeez, a poor bloody bear was in the cage, wearing some sort of tutu. It had a chain around its neck, music was playing and the poor bloody creature was being made to dance by a man poking it with a stick. It was appalling, I couldn't believe what I was seeing. Surely this wasn't legal?

We entered deeper into the fair, deeper into this alien world. There were the usual candy floss stalls, turkey leg stands (they love a turkey leg in Florida), dodgy looking rides, dodgy looking humans! We stood out as 'outsiders'.

A large sign outside a massive tent greeted us, 'COME ON IN, SEE THE ODDITIES OF THE WORLD'. We were intrigued, paid our two dollar entrance (per person) and in we trotted. It was like stepping into a movie set. Quite bizarre. There were different smaller tents inside, each requiring a dollar per look to see the oddities.

A three-headed snake (dead, not sure if it was ever alive!) Apparently the world's smallest horse (to be fair it was VERY small), stood still and sad inside a little crate of hay. Harvey loved the horse and Daisy tried to poke it's eye and then moo'd at it, poor thing! Aborted Siamese twins in a jar of pickle I guess (eww). A tattooed man who looked like a lizard, Daisy moo'd at him too (his days were numbered in the fair, it's not that unusual nowadays, just go into town on Saturday in the summer and see tattoos everywhere).

Then, the *piece de resistance*, requiring an extra three dollars a look, the world's smallest woman. I had to pay! Tentatively looking inside, there sitting on a little box, inside a crate (they like their crates) was a woman who it turned out was in her sixties, a grandmother from Barbados if I recall correctly. She was surrounded by photos of her family. She was sat with a radio playing and was knitting. I didn't know what to do. Should I take a photo, no that's just bloody rude.

'Hello,' I said. 'How are you?'

She replied in a kind but 'can't be arsed' way. She explained she travelled with the fair for six months of the year and had done since she was in her twenties. It was her income, her family's income. I felt so bad so obviously I asked, 'Do you feel exploited?' The words coming from someone who had just paid x amount of dollars to gawp. What a sorry state of affairs. In a modern world this was still acceptable, still allowed, still an oddity!

We left the tent. I was so sad but also angry. Nick pointed out that we were just as bad as everyone else in the fair. I disagreed, I would never have gone in had I known, had I read the placards... or would I? I don't know, but I do know its not right, so I guess I'm a hypocrite.

Next, the wheel of death, yep, stupid red neck men on motorbikes going round and round in a cylinder with all the baying crowd hoping for a fall. To be honest, a fall would have made it a bit more interesting, not death but a little bit of an accident would have livened it up.

Finally, 'All the Creatures of the World'. Well this wasn't entirely true as it would have been a bit of a bigger ring fenced area, but nevertheless they had quite a collection in what I would consider 'an accident waiting to happen' sort of condition. A giraffe in a small pen, some pigs, goats, cows, horses, an anteater, a porcupine, monkeys, a toothless lion which was about one hundred years old, a toothless man with a whopping big snake around his neck, bugs in bottles, a camel to sit on. They were all there, all shackled, all prisoners. We had helped keep this fair alive by paying our entrance fees, we left, bewildered, upset and speechless.

So where I have digressed with this story is that although

it is not really about Daisy (although she was with us), indirectly it is about Daisy. She would have been an oddity back in the day had she survived her epilepsy with no drugs. She would have been stared at, well actually she is still stared at. She would possibly have been 'The worlds biggest baby'. Hmm, now there's a thought!

Chapter Forty

Sleep... Nah!

So I have always loved my bed, who doesn't? I will tell you who, Daisy. The problem is not getting her to sleep, melatonin does that bit for me. No, it's the staying asleep that's the problem. I don't think in fourteen years that I have had a full night's uninterrupted sleep. It's not just the early mornings that are the issue. I can cope with them. It's the constant two hourly awakenings.

There is no explanation from the medics whose doors I have battered down over the years for answers, Daisy just cannot manage to sleep for prolong periods. Is the problem me? I sleep with her, firstly, because I am petrified she will die of a seizure in bed and secondly, it is so much easier to shove her back down when your drunk on lack of sleep, so could it be me that wakes her? Nick says I'm hot in bed (ooh er) maybe it is me.

We use the opportunity of a house move to make a bold decision to finally put Daisy in her own room. Designing her bedroom to be just off our bedroom we take the plunge and begin the transition. An epilepsy monitor is set and placed under the mattress, a monitor is set to watch her sleep. We are set up for the excitement of uninterrupted nights. It does go a lot easier than ever imagined and Daisy was not phased by not having me to pin down in the nights with her chunky thighs. I bet you are all waiting for me to say, it was me all along, and she now sleeps twelve hours a night. Alas, no, Daisy just cannot sleep.

I now have to get out of bed every two hours and that's on a good night. I scream, swear, pin her down and try to re-drug her. I try everything, have tried everything, so now its just accepted. Sleep is for the weak and bags under my eyes are now to be renamed suitcases.

Chapter Forty-One
Fifteen

Without doubt, the worst year of Daisy's (and our families) life.

Cleaning Daisy's teeth has never been easy, sometimes pretty impossible, but I have always tried my absolute best even if by just putting some toothpaste on a flannel and sweeping across her teeth in the hope I don't lose a finger or two. She has never missed a dental appointment and religiously we have turned up every six months to endure the torture of pinning Daisy in a dental chair, sitting on her and grappling to open her mouth in the hope that the dental team can examine.

Obviously, most times it is an almost impossible task but the teams always seemed happy with what they saw and never had concerns. I was always a bit obsessed and worried by Daisy's teeth and so once she reached the age of about ten/eleven I asked if thorough examinations could be done under general anaesthetic, linking them in with other procedures that were inevitable. It was agreed, and Daisy had three full checkups under a GA between the ages of ten and fourteen. They resulted in some fillings, one extraction and a coating of her biting surfaces to protect teeth. It was the best I could do for her.

During the spring of 2017, I noticed Daisy had a preference to eat on one side of her mouth. She had no obvious pain, but it was enough to concern me. I contacted the dental hospital whom she was under (and had been since the age of five) and asked for her to be seen as they had seemed to have missed giving her a follow up appointment for nearly a year.

An appointment was offered, then cancelled, then re-offered. Anyhow, we eventually saw a dentist in the May 2017. The usual scenario unfolded. A separate room was cleared, Daisy was coaxed into sitting in a chair with all sorts of bribes, Fimbles, my phone, playing 'Fireflies', a dummy waving like a carrot on a stick, stage one sorted.

Next, we had to get her mouth open. I straddled her, a dental nurse held her one arm while I led across the other, most undignified but necessary, cruel to be kind and all that. The dentist, whom I must say was fab, then prized Daisy's stubborn mouth open using all sorts of tools, and all looked great apart from a front incisor that was decayed. It was enough evidence for her to request another GA. I agreed and felt relieved that I was doing my utmost to keep Daisy well and happy.

Let's skip to August. The date for the GA is given.

We arrived at the children's hospital fully prepared as always. Nick was working away in Sierra Leone, but Harvey was home from Uni, so he was my chosen (well only) aide. Pre-op questions had been completed, the bed had been arranged. I ask ed if I could take Daisy home at 7.00am the next morning (why spend the night in hospital if nothing is wrong?), promising I would not feed or water the Gremlin.

No sooner had we driven from the hospital grounds did we receive a call.

'Is that Daisy's Mum?' asked the caller. 'Sorry to call but the procedure for Daisy has to be cancelled for tomorrow as we have a staffing issue.'

I can't tell you how disappointed I was, but this was something I was used to. I expected it, as you can never rely on surgery until you're actually in theatre. We waited for the new date, all the while mindful that Daisy was still eating, normally I might add, on a preferred side of her mouth.

The post arrived on the doormat. The new date was for late September. The whole rigmarole began again.

Pre-op was straight forward, a visit to see the dentist who will perform the procedure was next, and Daisy wasn't very compliant. This female dentist was a little less tolerant than others, but I just went with the flow, pinning Daisy down so that the dentist could do a quick examination. She agreed that one of Daisy's front incisors looked decayed and possibly couldn't be saved. I told her my previous concerns and she agreed to see her in the morning. This time Nick was home so he was able to accompany me.

The following morning, we took Daisy for dental treatment I will never forget. She was so happy. I remember her sitting on the hospital bed in her side room, clapping, loving all the attention she was getting from Mum, Dad and big bruv. We were doing this in her best interest and she would soon be out of the anaesthetic and back home eating yum yums. Administering the anaesthetic actually went without incident. Nick, myself and Harvey went to the café and got a coffee.

It was three and a half hours before we received a call. I assumed she might have had a seizure. I wasn't too concerned about this as it had happened many times before under GA. We walked into recovery. Daisy had two staff members with her. They were trying to wake her. We walked over. I don't think I will ever forget seeing her face that day. She was unrecognisable. Her beautiful face was covered in blood, grossly swollen just indescribable. She wouldn't wake at first so they put a mask on her. It took a while and then all hell broke loose. She woke, so confused, clearly in absolute agony, traumatised.

I asked what had happened and a nurse spoke to me. 'Twenty-one removed,' she said.

Nick and I both naively assumed she meant number twenty-one tooth had been removed so we asked her to clarify.

'They have removed twenty-one teeth,' she re-iterated.

I nearly passed out. I felt sick, couldn't hold in my burning tears. Daisy was escaping the room, confused, falling, distressed. My heart was broken.

The dentist came from theatre and matter of factly explained (although I wasn't fully listening) that she felt Daisy's teeth had too many cavities and, in her judgement, and to prevent further GA's, she took the decision to remove all but six teeth. Her decision! She removed twenty-one teeth from a fifteen-year-old-girl without consulting the parents, without considering the consequences, without fully understanding how this would affect Daisy. My mind is still struggling to this day with that dentist's blasé attitude to the life.

Back on the ward, Daisy was absolutely unmanageable, it was chilling, unforgivable. Nick, Harvey and I were just speechless. We couldn't comfort Daisy, she wouldn't let us hold her, touch her, go near her, but she was in the most unimaginable pain. We decided the best place for her was home. She would be surrounded by her special 'things', familiar sights. We asked to discharge her.

'The dentist needs to come and see her before discharge,' a kind, very sympathetic nurse remarked. 'I will call her.'

Time passed.

Then, in swanned the dentist (with her in-offensive side-kick who was mute). Full make-up, full mouth of teeth. I was and still am fucking furious, words were stuck in my throat.

I stared out of the window. I still regret not flying across the bed and knocking her through the door. It would have been worth the probable prison stint. This woman, with no thought for how we could manage Daisy; how her epilepsy would be managed, how she would eat, recover, smile, look. No thoughts.

Whether it is right or wrong (yes, I know its wrong), all I had to cling to and what made it easier to care for Daisy was her gorgeous little face, before the extraction of her looks. That's all I had to give me some normality. It was easier to love her because she was so beautiful... not any more! This poor girl now had a gummy inverted face, blood soaked, pitiful, unjust.

'Mum, she can always have dentures,' were the most unbelievable words that left that woman's mouth. 'She will soon be eating chicken nuggets,' came next.

We just stared at her, all three of us. All three of us, stunned and silent. She really had no idea what she had just done, no idea.

We discharged Daisy, were told to buy some paracetamol and ibuprofen. We took her home. She would be safe with us. I have never cried so much, ever, I still do cry. I'm crying now while recalling this.

The next days and weeks were a blur. Doctors were called out to try to ease the pain Daisy was enduring, the many different doctors that saw Daisy could not believe what had happened, had never come across such barbaric treatment and those were the words of the many medics we saw following surgery, as Daisy had to be prescribed morphine for the pain.

We even had a home visit by the lead consultant from the dental hospital. She saw the agony in Daisy's eyes. She knew what had happened was wrong. Apologies were offered, to this day they have never been accepted.

For three weeks no food entered Daisy's mouth, how could she trust me? How could she allow me to feed her? Medication was missed, seizures were continuous, the only way to get her to drink was to syringe fluids into her by pinning her down. Such an awful time for her. Her mouth was covered in cuts, sores, cold sores. Her face was double its normal size.

Hospital doctors wanted her to be admitted to control her pain, but I just couldn't bear to see the panic in her eyes. I would just have to manage her myself and do my utmost to make her comfortable.

What happened to Daisy that day changed her forever. Took away that little bit of independence of finger feeding that she had. Robbed her of her looks, stole the trust she had in me. Would this have ever happened to a fifteen-year-old girl if she was 'normal'? The answer is NO.

So, when told 'Daisy can have dentures', clearly the dentist didn't know Daisy's background, hadn't researched her case. Daisy could never be fitted or wear dentures, it would be like expecting a baby to wear them, it would never happen.

There was never any appreciation for Daisy's complicated condition, no understanding of how difficult caring for her on even 'good days' was and definitely no regard for the future management of medicating and feeding of Daisy and controlling the undisputed pain that followed the hideous removal of her teeth.

The suffering lasted a long time. Daisy struggled so much and I would have done anything for her to ease her torture. If only the dentist had consulted us, if only she had spoken to us, if only...

But, as I said to the complaints panel many months later, its too late now, the damage is done, you can't put them back so we had to do what we could to help Daisy adapt and move on. It was too late for her. Her diet became soft, no more stealing steaks for this little madam. Pringles were hidden, that would just be cruel if she'd seen them, thankfully Quavers melt so she could still enjoy something from her past. I even allowed her bloody Wotsits. Jeez the mess she makes with them, but to see the pure enjoyment was worth the orange clothes, furniture and walls!

I became a bit of a (rubbish) chef, making soft little parcels of food that she could pick up and feed herself as she refused to allow any sort of utensil to go near her. As time went by, her mouth started to heal, but it took many many months, she lost a huge amount of weight, some would say that was a good thing, but under the circumstances and the way it was lost was unhealthy and she must have felt so weak and crap.

Every day since that summer is a reminder whenever I look at Daisy. I think of it all the time and it breaks my heart. I guess I let Daisy down by not being more thorough with her tooth care (I clearly didn't do enough brushing), but it was never easy. I did what I could but I also trusted and believed that the measures I took were enough. If I had any doubts that I was failing Daisy I would have absolutely changed her oral care, but I was always told I was doing a good job.

But what hurts me the most is that still, in modern society, the medical professionals think it is OK to do a procedure so inhumane to a disabled person that would never even be considered on a person with any sort of what they consider 'quality of life'. Will times change? Sadly no, I don't think they will.

Chapter Forty-Two

Sixteen

I have never enjoyed Daisy's birthdays. They always remind me of what should've been, what could've been. Her sixteenth was particularly tough for me. I was still raw with the emotions of the trauma she had gone through and was still trying to accept her physical changes, trying not to get upset when I saw her smile at me so innocently through a smile that looked like an old lady's. That was hard, really hard, and still is. No one will ever know the hurt and guilt I feel.

How many mum's buy their sixteen-year-old daughter a few animal picture books and a replacement Teletubby for their milestone birthday, I'm guessing very few. This was the reality of Daisy's sixteenth. Of course, I wanted to be taking her on a girly shopping trip, maybe treat her to her first designer handbag, first pair of Louboutins, first Tiffany gift, alas it wasn't to be. I know that all sounds so fickle, but its what I wanted for Daisy.

Who knows, she might have been a proper tomboy. Nevertheless, I had my dreams for her like any mother and particularly on her sixteenth birthday I felt I was grieving for the life Daisy didn't have. I also felt utter sadness at not giving Nick the daughter he could spoil, protect and one day walk down the aisle, or the sister Harvey could bicker with and annoy. It was all far more real for some strange reason when she turned sixteen and it was hard for me to smile. Would I ever be happy?

So, with my miserable face grimacing and forcing myself to do the right thing and go through the motions, for her sixteenth she had a cake (obvs Colin the Caterpillar) which I blew the candles out on while on FaceTime so Nick could join in the singing from Sierra Leone, umpteen, no actually hundreds of renditions of 'Happy Birthday to You'. A visit to a carvery that required precision timing, seating and feeding and yep, that was it, a cheap date. Milestone over.

Chapter Forty-Three
Christmas Concert

Daisy has been in school since the age of three, so there have been a lot of school concerts we have had the agonising pleasure of sitting through. In the early days she was always an angel, I guess her cuteness and long blonde hair lent itself to the role, however it got more and more difficult as she got older to buy angel fancy dress outfits for a 'well covered' young lady!

Teachers don't consider this when you get the slip of paper home saying DAISY WILL BE A DISNEY PRINCESS, PLEASE PROVIDE A SUITABLE OUTFIT. Great if she's your average-sized princess, but not so great when she's the size of a small principality.

Over the years she has been a snowflake (just wore white, easy), a couple fairy's and angels (same outfit with alterations), a tree (she looked more like a Brussels sprout), a cow (went as herself, I jest, that was an easy one, pjs), a mouse (with no whiskers, no ears and no tail, basically just a grey blob), a queen (no crown, no skirt, just a queen in her civvies), and in the latter years a guitar (really!) and a star (just wore yellow... well, I tried).

Concerts have always been cringy. I am sure I am not alone in hating attending them, who really wants to see other children show off, not me that's for sure. I have sat with my hands in front of my eyes as Daisy has pushed a king off the stage, pushed a teacher off the stage, hit the mayor in the audience, hit the head teacher (that was funny), sat on the entrance to the stage refusing to move, had kicking tantrums, screaming tantrums, the list goes on and on.

Will I miss school concerts? A big fat nope!

Chapter Forty-Four
Seventeen

Never move house when you have a disabled child, that's the advice I would now comfortably offer anyone thinking of moving. We only moved from one county to a neighbouring county, just a twenty minutes drive. What were we thinking?!

It should have been a straightforward process as I had given ample notice to social services, but we had an absolutely hellish time. The system is appalling, something that should be streamlined and stress free caused me to have a near breakdown.

My nightmare started when Daisy had an anti-epilepsy medication removed abruptly following a period of nasty seizures. A new medication was introduced, then removed. It was a horrid time. Anyhow, what followed was non convulsive status (a period of intermittent seizure activity with minimal or no motor movements and an alteration of consciousness) and then Daisy being non textbook followed the episode with a complete manic episode lasting what felt like weeks.

Due to our recent move I was without help. I had no carers, no respite, nobody. Daisy would spend her days hitting her head, punching her nose, screaming, high shrill screaming, stripping, removing nappy (clean or soiled). It was endless. She didn't sleep for four whole days and nights, it was on the fourth night that I couldn't take it anymore.

It was 3.00am on a Saturday and I called social services, something I would never do because the social workers are usually either on the sick or in a meeting. I was put through to a duty officer. Giving her Daisy's details, condition, my worries, etc.

'Are you thinking of hurting Daisy or yourself?' was the initial reply from the duty social worker.

'No,' was my innocent reply.

'Then you need to call an on-call doctor' was the blasé response.

Remember, it's 3.00am, Daisy was climbing the walls and I was beside myself.

I called the doctor's.

'I need to see a doctor, its urgent,' I said through tears streaming down my ugly face.

'What's the emergency?'

I explained my situation, the epilepsy saga, nutty psycho child, no sleep, needing help, I was desperate.

'You will need to contact social services!' the doctor exclaimed.

I hung up. I sat for an age just crying. Daisy came into me with her nappy in her mouth. I laughed, probably out of hysteria. Fresh nappy fight, screams, self harm (her not me). I'd had it.

At 4am I plonked Daisy in the car and we drove to the out of hours surgery. I didn't have an appointment and the shirty receptionist attitude reflected this, but there was no one there apart from a guy outside high on Spice, pissing against a car tyre, nice! So Miss Snooty Pants let me in.

A doctor appeared. *Quite old for a doc,* I thought. *Probably doing a bit on the side to top up his pension and ex wives* (my mind is an odd one). He calls Daisy's name over a speaker, even though we were the only ones in the room, here we go, this will be fun.

We entered his lair. I started to tell the story of the past few days. Daisy didn't disappoint. The room was literally trashed. Good girl, he should listen. He got on the phone once he had grappled the lead from Daisy's mouth. He frantically typed me a letter eager to get us out of the room.

'Take this to Children's Assessment Unit,' exasperated and worried words exit his mouth. 'Take care,' he said – kind words not usually spoken to me.

We drove to the Assessment Unit, where they were waiting. Daisy was like a tornado. The ward literally did not know what had hit them. A side room was soon found for us and we were escorted, but only after Daisy had sat butt naked in the corridor of the ward for a good half hour. Nurses just stared. After coaxing Daisy into her 'cell' I closed the door and just stared at her, wondering what would become of her.

As the sun rose, a doctor entered the room. Daisy was obviously naked. What's the point of trying to dress her, she just keeps ripping her clothes. I try to cover her boobies, but she's having none of it, so I let them air themselves. The many questions begin. I'm tired, upset, exhausted, fearful, a rubbish mother, angry, irritated and just want to explode. I can't bear that I have to go through all the quizzing and the constant repeating of myself, I fear I may self combust.

I'm going to spare you the next of many many hours as everything they try to give Daisy doesn't work. She's as strong as an ox and probably needed a horse tranquilliser, but I suppose I would've needed a vet for that. Next time I will consider.

Guess who turned up when I look like a fucking bag of shit, Mr Nice. He ordered me to go home. I kept refusing but I was almost kicked out of the hospital. He told me he would sort care out for Daisy, but presently he thought I needed sleep. *He is a god*, I thought. I looked at Daisy as I left, her wiring all wrong, eyes like saucers. I felt so, so sad for her but also hated what she was doing to me.

As I drove home to sleep, I thought about crashing the car. I thought about what the social services spokesperson had asked me, should I? Then tears came again (told you I was close to a breakdown), how bloody selfish would that have been? Nick would have been lumbered, yes lumbered, with Daisy and I would be dead, but free!

I know I'm a horrible human, but I could never have done that to Nick or left Daisy and Harvey. How would Nick have coped, he couldn't, could he? Would he/she/they be better off without me? Tough if the answer is yes, I ain't going nowhere.

I don't know why I bothered going home that night. I didn't sleep, just lay there feeling sorry for myself. But I did get to shower, put on some make-up and return to the hospital at 6.30am.

I tentatively entered the ward, gave my name on the intercom and was almost thrust into Daisy's cell. Two guards were shell-shocked. Daisy was naked (shock). There were padded mattresses on the floor, wrapped around the bed rails and the two guards/staff members looked broken. They explained she had been administered several sedatives and all of which had failed. Daisy grinned at me with her gummy chops. Oh Daisy!

The outcome of the hospital stay was that a fabulous, quite dishy palliative care doctor, who had tried to get me some respite with the hospice (but failed) offered us to try a drug called levomepromazine. It is usually given as end of life pain and or anxiety relief, but it can be given for heavy sedation. Worth a try? Too bloody right. It was a revelation. Just 0.5ml of the wonderful solution was administered and within an hour Daisy slept like a little baby, not for hours but she slept! I lay beside her, stroked her, my heart bleeding, this drug could be our saviour. Now I needed to get it on her bloody prescription.

Over the next few days, Daisy started to sleep much better, still waking every night several times but at least she slept some of the time. Life started getting easier again. Whenever I sat in the tearoom at work and anyone dared to say they were tired, I would just look up from the usual garbage I was reading and just smirked. They had no idea, absolutely no idea.

So, like I said at the beginning, don't move house when your child is disabled. There is no transition of services, everyone passes the buck, no one cares, no one takes responsibility, no one helps you, you are not their problem anymore. I was on my own and could have easily become a statistic, a forgotten bit of bad news: 'Mother kills herself and child'. But annoyingly I couldn't kill a cockroach so Daisy is lucky I guess, if lucky is the correct choice of word.

Chapter Forty-Five
Eighteen

On the day of Daisy's eighteenth birthday, all respite stopped. She was now an adult in the eyes of the authorities and no longer Child Services problem (I bet there was a hell of celebration behind the closed doors of social services). No respite, no hospice, no help. There was supposed to be a streamlined transition from child to adult (a bit like the moving house transition), but that didn't happen and from speaking to countless 'professionals' it rarely does.

Ty Hafan Children's hospice had Daisy just a week before her eighteenth so that Nick and I could have one final short holiday. We chose Qatar as our destination. Nice. Daisy had the best time while we were gone. Spoilt rotten, constant attention, constant love and care. She would miss the place. So sad her care there couldn't continue.

Social Services were now struggling to find me respite. There is just not a facility for an 'adult' like Daisy. The newly appointed social worker who insisted her role was only temporary, explained to me that it would be very difficult for them to offer me any sort of respite so I had to play the 'if you cant offer me respite I cannot continue to care for Daisy' card. I hated having to use this strategy, but it's fact, if I can't have a night off now and again, how can I be expected to continue with caring for Daisy? I'm not getting any younger that's for sure. I became a regular nag, emails, voice messages, texts, more emails, more voicemails. This is what you have to do to get any help, become unliked, a nuisance. It worked. A place was found.

A private facility that took disabled adults eighteen to twenty-five years of age was suggested to be the most suitable setting for Daisy's next care package. I was given all the details. It was out of county, but not too far to drive and I was happy to do the toing and froing. It sounded great, with a maximum of three residents at a time, a home from home, fab! All the necessary paperwork was completed. School visits were carried out by the staff from the home and we were good to go.

Daisy was initially offered two nights a month with the intention of it increasing to five, great I thought, just perfect. Daisy went for a tea visit to let the staff get used to her and all seemed to go well. Her first overnight soon came along. As was expected, my anxiety levels reached head bursting proportions but it seemed to go 'OK', not great, just OK. I told myself the staff would get used to her stubborn ways after all you really do need the patience of a saint with Daisy and it really is a test when caring for her. Let's just say maybe not all the staff were saints!

Over the next few months, the visits became very tense. I received many phone calls from the manager explaining different incidents. Daisy had on one occasion, in the managers words, 'had a member of staff pinned against a wall' (that just could never have happened), thrown her food across the room (OK, that probably happened but there would have been a good reason – too hot, staff member not giving her full attention when feeding her, etc, etc.), attacking staff (not true, pushing away and the odd slap, but she hasn't got the intelligence to attack).

I had so many calls lecturing me on Daisy's apparent unmanageable behaviours.

Duh! That's why she is in your care, I thought to myself, but as the saying goes I chose not to bite my nose off to spite my face and kept quiet just apologising on Daisy's behalf.

Each visit I worried. Each visit became a concern. The staff just were not up to a Daisy. They were happy to take the money from the council (undoubtably a huge sum), but not happy to endure the difficult little ways my petal had. The inevitable crunch came. Daisy was for want of a better word, expelled from the care home. Bloody great, now what.

Social services were at a loss, so I went down the route of finding my own carers. People I could trust, people who *I* felt could understand Daisy and manage her.

There have been many girls caring for Daisy over the years, Jemima, Lisa, Adele, to name a few of the good ones, but one in particular has been a constant in Daisy's life since about the age of six if I can recall back that far. She has looked after Daisy like she were her own. She gets Daisy and Daisy gets her. She left us for a while to have her own children (rude) but she soon came back on the radar and now gets her weekly fix of Daisy by having her overnight for me.

Sorreya, a pain in the arse, but an absolute diamond, gobby, loud but a great human (hope she doesn't read this her head will swell). So, that's where we are now, back to having Sorreya care for Daisy. She is our respite and we thank her.

The next chapter in Daisy's life will soon be upon us though and it's a chapter I am both excited about, but also dreading. It's something I have always said would never happen but I feel our hand has almost been forced as we have little options open to us. It's been such a difficult decision but we feel (hope) we are doing the right thing by Daisy

When Daisy finishes school in July that's it. There is no place in our hometown for Daisy to 'go' on a day to day basis to get a structured day. Daisy needs routine. She needs to continue with sensory education, she needs intensive interaction and we need respite to continue in the future. I don't want her days to be just going for a walk in the park or to a day centre every day with no end purpose. Daisy needs more. Daisy deserves more.

Careers Wales (yes, read correctly) have been involved with us for a while now and their help and advice has been amazing. Options have been put on the table, we as a family have visited the options (one quite local to us you wouldn't put a dog in, needs a Panorama Investigation in my opinion but I won't go there) and we have decided on the most incredible next step in Daisy's life.

Daisy will be going (subject to funding from the Welsh government) to Star College in Cheltenham in September 2020. Daisy in College, I never thought those words would exit my lips. Let that sink in, Daisy in College, wow. The college is INCREDIBLE. Nick and I have been on two visits now and are blown away. The care and dedication the staff have will without doubt give Daisy the best next three years she could hope for, more attention than you can shake a stick at, more expertise than she could ever dream of, more help than we could wish for. We are so excited but also so damn nervous. We know it's the right step, we know its for the best but how will we (but especially me) cope?

The answer is, I don't know and I feel sick thinking about it but I am confident this is the right next step. If it's not, Daisy will return to me and I will manage, always will. I will just need a bit more juice and let's remember it's just three years, just three long years.

So, that's it, you're up to date. It's now 2020 and coronavirus has invaded the world. Daisy is obviously oblivious, still going to school (thank God I'm a key worker in the NHS. Let me just prop up my halo while you clap for me). Nick is stuck in Guinea, West Africa (did he even try to get an emergency flight home, is he even on the Foreign Office Rescue List? Hmmmm).

Lockdown has kicked me up the bum to finish the book (cheers COVID-19). Its only taken about ten years! Daisy's new chapter in her life will hopefully be starting in September subject to the bloody virus not fucking it all up (that will be just typical). Will I cope without her? I don't think so. Will I miss her? Hell yes. Will I have guilt? Always. I will see her every week, without fail. I will worry every day, but Nick and I know from that initial visit that what we are doing is out of a love so deep that we have to allow her to at least experience something that we can't give her. I'm confident she will be happy, if not, I will bring her home, what I will do with her who knows but I guess that is something time will answer.

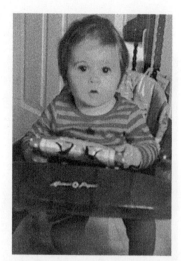

Danger Girl, 16 months old

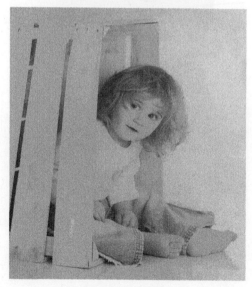

2 years and 3 months

Just eaten a lump of mud, aged 3

Trying to look like a happy family, 2003

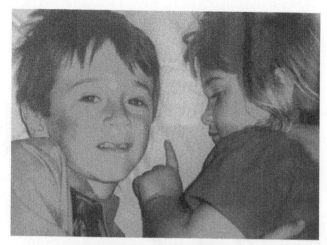

Harvey and Daisy, aged 4

First school concert, aged 4

Jaws ride, Florida, aged 6

Aged 8

Florida, aged 9

Portugal, aged 10

Florida, aged 11

Aged 13

Florida, aged 13

Aged 14

Daisy loves water, aged 14

She really does, aged 14

Aged 15

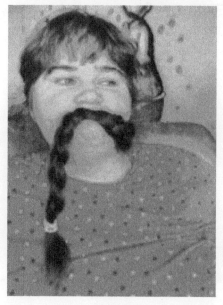

Aged 16

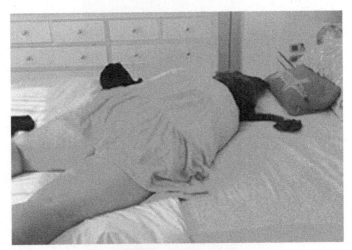

Melting in the heat, aged 17

18ᵗʰ birthday

Part Two

These following pages are a snapshot of my, our, daily life. What really happens daily, weekly in the life caring for a 'Daisy'. They are excerpts from my previous blog and are written to tell it as it is.

Daisy is fifteen years old and cannot talk. In fact, Daisy can't do most things we all take for granted. You see, although physically she is a big fifteen year-old girl, mentally she is ten months old. Imagine what that's like!

If I had a pound for every time I've uttered the words 'Daisy can't talk' I'd be very rich indeed, but the 'not talking' is just a small fragment of her problems.

Daisy is classed as PMLD which to most of the population means very little but to those thrust into the world of 'special needs' means Profound Multiple Learning Difficulties.

She has never been given a 'real' diagnosis and throughout the years we have had umpteen 'syndromes' thrown into the pot. Retts, Angleman, Prada-Willi, the list goes on and on. Google was needed for all of them, none of them came up trumps. Daisy is unable to communicate or understand language and through her frustrations can get a tad agitated! She lives in a world that doesn't tolerate or understand. Daisy has no clue when people stare, laugh, judge, but I (we) do and I am so sad for the life I have given her.

Daisy has refractory epilepsy, suffering seizures every two to three weeks. She will never have a boyfriend, husband, lover (why did I choose that order?). She will never steal my clothes, handbags or make-up. Will never ask for an iPad or iPhone for her birthday. Never play her music too loud (Harvey, are you reading this?), never get drunk (Harvey, are you reading this?). Many parents would think these are blessings, but not me. I'd love her to do all the above and more.

This is about Daisy's day-to-day life and the struggles we face as a family (well, actually the struggles *I* face, everyone else has buggered off) just trying to lead at best a 'normal' life. I may not always be politically correct, so please don't take offence, they are only words! I hope it will show readers that life can be shitty at times, but if you can laugh at adversity it can – with the help of wine and chocolate – be tolerable... just!

About Me

I'm a wife and mum of two. My hubby Nick works in West Africa and pops home every six weeks to see me. My son Harvey is a first year law student at the University of Birmingham, a clever boy who obviously takes after me!

Me, I work (use the term loosely) in hospital pharmacy and try to make clinical trials run nice and smoothly.

I love all trash reality *TV, TOWIE, Love Island, Ex on the Beach, Housewives* of just about everywhere... you get the picture. I also love fashion, shopping, spending my husband's money, wine, gin, crisps and chocolate.

Daisy has consumed my life for the last fifteen years, I've cried (a lot), laughed, worried and been immensely frustrated by all that comes with having a 'special needs child', but I don't let her disability stop me being me and I never will.

March 17th
First Blog

So, this is my first blog and I've chosen a crappy day to write it. I should be in work. Daisy should be in school and at quarter past three I should be having respite; somehow, things never seem to go to plan for me though. Seizures ruin everything!

I'm sitting here on the sofa in the kitchen, looking at Daisy all snuggled up and out for the count, but all I'm thinking instead of being filled with sadness is that I will be up all bloody night as she will recover at about 2:00am, that's how it works with epilepsy, it sucks!

First seizure was at 2:15am, then at 6:25am, and then at 10:15am (might I add, just as the DNA results were being announced by Jeremy Kyle). There have been no more today so I am hopeful that it is over, however, Daisy has been post-ictal all day so I am pretty confident that come two am she will be as bright as a button and I will want to kill!

I'm feeling pretty sorry for myself.

March 19th

Good Morning, I Hope...

So, my prediction was almost spot on. Daisy woke at 1.40am. She was pointing to the TV in her room and bashing her nose, but I was having none of it. This is her way of communicating, she has learned that the harder she bashes her nose the quicker she will get what she wants. Clever, I guess, but today I'm not in the mood! So my grumpy bear growl greets her.

She follows me into my bed and taking up a central position lay across most of the bed. I hate her getting into my bed because it inevitably means I will have to change all the bedding in the morning due to nappy leakage, but I need sleep so in she gets. I perched into a corner with my head on the edge of the bedside table hoping that she would soon settle back off to sleep. I daren't move, I must not wake her. I need sleep.

My legs are crushed, arm is dead and neck is cricked, but I'm feeling pretty happy because at least she went back to the land of nod for a couple of hours and its now 5.30am! Woohoo!

Daisy isn't particularly happy this morning... no sounds yet. Usually I get a 'moo' or 'quack' if she see's something on the TV, never a cow or duck I hasten to say, but so far this morning nothing.

I prepare her breakfast and always feel like I'm serving up food for the animals in the zoo. Chopped up cereal bar, dry cereal, raisins, toast, and her 'special' teacake laced with anti-epilepsy medication – yum! – all cut into bite sized pieces so that she can finger feed herself.

I've laid it out in front of Her Majesty, but she looks in disgust and points to the cupboard. I know what she wants, Quavers! Another learned behaviour. Daisy knows I will give in, as soon as she receives the Quavers she starts to eat her breakfast.

It's not easy with a child like Daisy, she doesn't watch films, can't play, can't use crayons or read, can't do much apart from eat and shit, so my options are limited to a drive in the car or a walk, but its always raining!

The day has been a day of changing huge nappies, coaxing Daisy to take medication, endless episodes of crappy CBeebies and boredom. I can't wait for what tomorrow brings.

Later that day

Great sleep. Daisy woke at 11.00pm, 1.30am, 2.15am, 3.00am and 4.20am at which point I gave in, she won! I want to kill!

I did try all sorts of tactics, cuddles (she is not a fan), shouting (she doesn't care), ignoring her (she just pulls and prods me). TV went on at 4.00am, but by 4.20am she wanted food so started her annoying prodding, it's at that point I realised she had pooped, great!

All cleaned up, we are now downstairs and I have fed my angel and laced her food with the first part of her medication.

It's still only 5.15am and I have that sinking feeling – how am I going to get through the next fourteen hours? But for now, beds need changing and Daisy needs a bath, so that's one hour sorted – only thirteen left.

Same day – bedtime

I'm so glad it's time for bed. I feel like I have jet lag and the furthest I've been today is the garage up the road!

Daisy decided to go on a crash diet today so has eaten nothing of any substance. Breakfast was her only 'proper' meal, after that it was all downhill. Often after nasty seizures she loses her appetite so I'm not too worried but it has proven difficult to administer her medication. I had to straddle her and trap her head between my knees to get her medication in, cruel to be kind and all that!

She has also been very hyper with manic episodes of laughter which is not nice to see but again is a usual trait after seizures; she will often switch from being subdued to manic to aggressive and then back to normal, whatever 'normal' is?

So to say I'm glad it's bedtime is an understatement! Roll on tomorrow, let's just hope it doesn't start too early in the morning!

March 20th

I Also Hate Mondays...

Well that wasn't a successful night either! Daisy was so restless, taking her nightie off and waving her nappy like a flag. I've lost count how many times I tried to settle her. At 2.00am I joined her in her bed (always a mistake) and she fell quickly back to sleep, with me as her pillow. So she was comfy and I just lay there with her twitching and breathing in my face, willing the birds to sing to tell me it was morning.

Be careful what you wish for! Her sleeping didn't last long and by 4.20am she had won again. Worryingly she was laughing out loud, not a good sign. To make matters worse, this morning Daisy has a heavy cold. She cannot blow her nose so tusks keep appearing and you have to be quick to catch them.

I am preparing myself to go to battle in a minute and give her medication. I can tell by her mood that she is going to resist, but I also need to give her Calpol so I need to just bite the bullet.

Teletubbies has just come on TV so there is a smile on her face, now is the time to strike with her meds... bingo!

Daisy is quite confused still and keeps wandering around the house, but on the whole she is OK. Dressing for school goes smoothly, although I have put four nappies on her by

8am as she keeps ripping the sides; the more I shout the more she does it... arghhh!

Transport arrives for school. And breathe.

Later...

Daisy left for school this morning and appeared unsteady and confused, but happy. This is common after seizures that affect a certain part of the brain and each day she improves, but it does take a while.

When she returned from school at 4.00pm, Daisy still seemed 'away with the fairies'. She was trying to drink out of her non-spill cup but it was upside down! She sat in the middle of the kitchen and then licked the corner of the sofa?

I opened up her school diary and did chuckle. I'm guessing (hoping) it was a slip of the pen but her teacher had written: 'Daisy has been very confused today, we have tried to keep the classroom calm to prevent her from getting executed.' I am hoping she meant to say excited!

March 21st

Four is the New Six...

This is getting ridiculous. How am I supposed to function on such little sleep? I can't even get angry with Daisy at the moment because firstly I don't have the energy, and secondly she is in cloud cuckoo land – a completely different world to me (although, some would disagree)!

I won't bore you with how many times she woke last night, but suffice to say we were sat downstairs at 4:30am. Daisy grinning and still manic. Me, in a zombie state!

I thought adding a little bit of anti-psychotic to her evening meds would help (they are prescribed, I don't just buy from a dodgy site), but no difference noted. Her brain is a law unto itself.

Morning routine runs smoothly. Off to school and work we go. I've had a difficult day in work due to the overwhelming need to sleep, so I prepare Daisy's tea and wait for her transport to bring her home.

I have fifteen minutes to go, my eyes are closing... the doorbell rings and I dart off the sofa – I never fall asleep, but believe me, I needed that fifteen minute snooze. Bring it on Roo!

Daisy seems less confused and does eat her tea, even

though each mouthful I feed her is followed by her putting her big toe in her mouth and chewing it! This is a game she loves, I have to wriggle her toe out of her tooth's clamp between spoonful's, not nice when it's covered in cottage pie.

I was a little sad reading Roo's school annual Governor';s report that was sent home in her bag this evening. Apparently 90% of pupils met their reading targets this year. This is a special school for children with severe learning difficulties, and reading this report hits home – Daisy is clearly in the other 10%! Exceptionally special in a special school, typical.

I'm hopeful she will sleep better tonight. I'm considering getting so plastered that I won't pay any attention to her if she wakes but I guess I'd better not, I will still need to care for her come the morning and its not nice with a hangover, believe me, not nice at all.

March 22nd

Always Flush After a Wee...

So I probably did drink too much last night and maybe slept through a couple of awakenings, but Daisy seemed un-phased by my shit parenting skills and managed to wake me at 1.40am and 4.30am. Strangely 4.30am now seems a reasonable time to be woken by a snot covered dummy hitting me on the forehead, and a wet nappy smell entering my nostrils.

I did attempt to redirect her back to bed, but she was having none of it. So downstairs we go and on goes the heating. It's just as well hubby is in Africa. He hates me advancing the heating, always telling me to just put a jumper on! As if!

Daisy seems much more 'with it' this morning so I'm feeling hopeful it will be an easy morning. Breakfast goes without a hitch, dressing her goes relatively smoothly – when I say relatively smoothly I do mean it took only three attempts to put her vest and shirt on as opposed to more!

She also only ripped one nappy, so happy days.

Taking advantage of her mood, I decided to shower while she was looking out of her bedroom window quacking at anything that went by. Forgetting momentarily that I had a 'Daisy' I was whisked into a world of soap suds and peace, then she appeared. I thought she had a marker pen (from where? Who knows!) in her mouth so I was whisked back to reality and shot out of the shower.

Shouting at her to drop the pen, as if I was shouting at a robber to 'drop the knife', she took it out of her mouth and threw it. Plop, straight into the toilet. If it had been a marker pen I wouldn't have been bothered, but of course it was my Dior mascara, only two weeks old. I did rescue it but it wasn't sealed quite enough so was mixed with wee, never to be used again. Moto, always flush after a wee!

Daisy had a good day at school, no incidents to report, phew!

Apart from my devastating mascara loss today has been a good one. Let's hope tonight follows the same pattern and the sleep fairy visits us both.

March 23rd

Nothing Like a Lie in!

Does 4.35am count as I lie in, I ask myself? After the week I've had the answer is yes!

Daisy slept quite well until 1.40am when I heard the heart sinking rattles of the bed rails as she shook them for attention.

I watched the monitor beside my bed for a few seconds to see if she would settle herself but no, she started to strip and so in I stumbled, refusing to greet her and in usual automated mode, re-dressed her, rammed a dummy in her mouth and gently lowered her to the pillow (and if you believe that you're an eejit!).

Back in bed, I lay watching her as the lights of the monitor flickered, fuck I want to throttle her, she's shaking the rail again; her eyes in the infrared light look like she's possessed, maybe she is, could that be it?

I'm expecting her head to spin any minute. I stomp back into her room but she immediately lies down. She knows her life is hanging in the balance. She sleeps! I don't, I'm now fully awake and willing myself to sleep. I'm counting how many hours I have until I wake, how many hours I've slept. Sheep are jumping over a gate and I'm counting them, but I'm still bloody awake. Then the 4.35am day starts and here we go again.

I want to watch the news but can't, Daisy rules. On goes Sky + and the endless episodes of *Teletubbies*. I transform into a model housewife; strip and wash her bedding, replace with fresh bedding, prepare breakfast, prepare medication, feed her breakfast – slowly, attempt to administer medication, and then give up trying to administer medication.

Attempt dressing her, give up trying to dress her. Attempt hair brushing, give up hair brushing. Re-try dressing, only manage the top half. Re-try medication, abandon medication. Re-try hair while singing Old MacDonald, success with hair. Re-try medication (lets sing Old MacDonald again), no success. Re-try bottom half of uniform, notice new nappy required, change nappy, bottom half of uniform on, success! Re-try medication with the bribe of a Jammy Dodger, refusal. Re-try with a Jammy Dodger and an Oreo, success.

Transport arrives, Daisy refuses to leave, so for the next seven to eight minutes I sing a musical medley while marching around the house with various toys waving from behind the door to entice her out, the tune to *EastEnders* finally wins her round. She can take no more and ups and goes with not a passing glance. Bye bye, petal!

School, done. Now off to work.

March 24th

Never Ever...

My head's spinning, boy I'm in a daze.
I feel isolated, don't want to communicate.
I'll take a shower, I will scour.
I will roam
To find peace of mind
The happy mind
I once owned.

10.45pm, 12.05am, 1.50am, 2.15am. TV on at 3.05am, downstairs 3.50am. How I didn't smother her, God only knows. Mind you, she's stronger than me so I would need quite a few Weetabix to 'do the job'!

She's happy, I'm irritated by her, she's smiling at me, I smile back (still don't like her though).

Yesterday in work I read a poster someone had put up raising awareness for autism through a 'fancy dress theme', great I thought but then the more I thought about it the more I felt jealous. Ridiculous isn't it, being jealous of parents with autistic children... what's wrong with me? My reasoning (to me) is simple, Daisy doesn't 'belong' in any group, whether it be autism, Downs, cerebral palsy, Retts, etc.

She has no link; she has no friends. In fact, since being a

170

toddler, she has never (let me think) no, never been invited to a birthday party and that breaks my heart. Having no diagnosis is very difficult. There are no answers and we as a family are just expected to 'get on with it'.

We are not experts in caring, and I certainly am no saint but my life has become this monotonous roundabout of just making sure Roo is kept content. I don't want her to be uncomfortable or unhappy or hungry or in pain, but because she can't communicate all my efforts are guess work and its tiresome, extremely tiresome. But, hey, onwards and upwards. It's Friday and that means curry.

Never ever have I felt so low
When you gonna take me out of this black hole?
Never ever have I felt so sad
The way I'm feeling, you got me feeling really bad.

March 25th

Bloody Hell, It's 5.30am!

I can't quite believe it, Daisy only woke once, around 2.00am. She has slept! Whoop whoop, clap clap!

Seeing 5.31am lit up on the bedside table – what joy! Maybe today will be a good day? I've actually been dreading today. You see, Daisy has no carers to help any more. I used to get help after school for two nights and on a Saturday, but Daisy finished the last two carers off! They just couldn't manage her!

Ridiculous, I know, but I had better not say too much as my gobby mouth could get me in trouble. I do get respite five nights a month, but the nights never come when you need them. This week is a great example.

I also feel incredibly anxious and guilty when I drop Daisy to respite. I really don't know if she's happy there. I hope so, but I'm just not comfortable.

Do others care for her kindly? Do they give her the attention she craves? Do they understand her? I know the answer is probably 'yes' to all my doubts, but it makes no difference to how I feel.

Daisy should be 'out with her mates' in town on a Saturday. She should be in MAC with a group of giggling girls trying on lipsticks and having slug-like eyebrows drawn on her face. She should be refusing to get out of bed, she should hate me (well she might, but I'll never know).

She should be crying over boys and crying over girls, but no. Today Daisy will be with me, her mum. Something a nearly sixteen-year-old girl would not do on a Saturday unless they were clothes shopping. I grieve for the girl I haven't got and then I feel guilty for wanting her to be different – but I do. I want her to be 'normal'.

People always say to me 'you wouldn't change her'. Yes, yes I would. In a heartbeat. I also feel so sad for the sister I have given her brother. He's missed out, that's heartbreaking. My husband doesn't have a daughter, he has a 'Roo'. A giant baby who wears nappies and sucks a dummy.

My anxiety has always been a hurdle with respite, but I am grateful and have to just accept that I need a break, but it is difficult.

So, my plans for today are, after the morning struggle to dress and medicate madam:

1. Take Daisy for a drive to Starbucks drive-through - she loves the ride, I love the coffee.
2. Wash her bedding, and – wait for it – hang it on the line!
3. Cut the lawns with my new Gtech cordless mower, no more shackled to a socket for me! (Daisy will shadow me the whole time, she loves the mower, and the Hoover, and will probably moo and quack at any passing dogs.)
4. Another drive in the car to collect a McDonalds (her treat for a Saturday), what a bad parent I am!
5. Medication-laced teacake

6. Take her to respite at 3.15pm.
7. Guilt, guilt, guilt.
8. Take my mother for a meal for Mother's Day.
9. Want to slit my throat after meal with Mother
10. Bed

Oh, shit, must go... Poo-tastrophy.

March 26th

A Lovely Bouquet...

Yesterday I had a phone call...

Interflora. I was actually at home cutting the grass. Daisy wouldn't come outside, so was watching from the window. Anyway, I answered the phone and a woman's voice asked, 'Hi, is that Mrs Rainey? I have a bouquet of flowers for you.'

'Ooh, lovely.'

'Do you live in a white house on a corner?'

'Yes, why?'

'Well, I'm outside the door. I've been ringing the bell and speaking to a young girl through the glass, but she won't answer. She is looking at me, staring, but ignoring me.'

Telling the woman I'd be right there, I ran inside and there was Daisy with her nose squeezed up to the door, dummy in mouth, oblivious. Not a clue! I answered the door and was handed the bouquet by a puzzled looking woman. Should I apologise? Should I be embarrassed? Nah, so taking the flowers and offering a hasty, 'Thank you' and then shut the door.

I'll enjoy the flowers and let the delivery woman think whatever she wants. It will give her something to talk about back at the office. It made me smile, but also made me so sad. Oh Daisy, what am I going to do with you?

March 27th

Silent...

Since coming home from school today, Daisy has been silent. Not a peep. No 'yum yums', 'da's', 'quack quacks', 'moo's', nothing. She's silent. Her hands are a purplish red, her skin mottled, cheeks crimson, skin dry, eyes sad.

All of this is usual, its become the norm. Due to frustrations with most medics over the years, I don't burden them with Daisy any more. Who wants to sit in a GP surgery with all the sick patient's judging you, as you try to prevent your little cherub from sitting on someone's lap, stealing crisps, pushing a child, pushing an adult, flashing her boobs, flashing her front bottom!

Not me, now I just manage Daisy and all the worrying and upsetting symptoms that come as part of the parcel of having her. Not a day goes by when I don't worry about her (and before you think it, no I don't have Munchausen by proxy).

So today, I have bathed her in a nice warm Jacuzzi to warm her hands and get her circulation going. I've massaged her chunky legs (makes her chuckle). moisturised her dry skin and I've tried to brighten those sad eyes by singing her favourite tunes (badly) whilst conditioning her beautiful Rapunzel hair.

I've administered her anti-epilepsy medication, sat on her

to give her some ibuprofen for suspected period pain (don't get me started on periods) and I've drugged her so that she can fall asleep (don't worry, it's legal).

I'm sitting watching her monitor now and she looks so peaceful. She's kicked the duvet off and is hopefully having happy dreams. I'd love to know what those dreams would be. She deserves the best ones, not dragons and monsters, but dreams of buying beautiful clothes, beautiful bags, diamonds and dating Jamie Dornan... just like my dreams!

March 28th

Three Kids And A Pigeon

11.00pm, 1am, 2.15am up at 4.45am. Bugger it, back to no sleep! Still, she's in a delightful mood today so I shouldn't grumble – should I? I can't blame Daisy for her early rise this morning, as I totally lay the blame on the effing wood pigeon that is nestled in the tree opposite our house.

It was still bloody dark when it started its hideous chirping and to add insult to injury, Daisy was mimicking the sound. I swear if I'd had a gun, I don't know who'd have been first to get the bullet. I'm guessing the bird, but Daisy would have been a close second.

There were more contenders for a bullet this morning. Three snotty kids on scooters that pass my house every morning at 8.15am. They always stop to see if Daisy is standing in the window and giggle if she is.

Bless her, she is unaware they are laughing at her. She just watches them and wiggles to the sound of their scooters going up and down the pavement, but I know they only stop to laugh... little bastards.

They sometimes get my, 'laugh again and I will break your legs' stare, but I try to rise above it. One day, all three may have to pay the price for daring to mock my little pet!

Maybe I could invite them in and Daisy could play with

them, now that would be fun. They wouldn't last five minutes, or maybe they will get the same treatment the wood pigeon will get tomorrow if it dares to wake madam. Who knows what the future of three kids and a pigeon will be?

March 29th

It's Rude to Stare.

11.45pm, 12.35am, 1.50am, 2.55am, 4.35am.

E ven the bloody birds weren't awake. I should have gone and shaken the trees to wake the bastards up.

Hospital appointment today, 9.00am. Daisy always has to have the first appointment. There are less targets for her to push over at that time and less glaring parents praying their little darlings don't end up the size of her.

Easy isn't it to say you're going to feed your child the healthiest of diets and provide them with all the opportunities for a healthy lifestyle? I have tried with Daisy and failed, one reason follows.

Many years ago, we were members of a certain well-known fancy shmamsy Leisure Club. I never really went for the gym side. I would just go for coffee. Expensive bloody coffee that membership became.

Nick and Harvey would have a great time and I resented them spending every horrid minute in that place. It reminded me of how different our family was becoming. Perfect beautiful families enjoying leisure time. Me trying to 'fit in', trying to lead the same lives as everyone else, except there was one flaw, Daisy!

Back to the appointment. Daisy was OK at the hospital,

just OK. Harvey came with me to help manage her and he was great (although he should have been studying). She took a while to get weighed, as everything is on her terms, so we had quite a wait.

There were the usual stares from the waiting room. One particular man is lucky I didn't tell him to 'stop fucking staring', as his eyes were transfixed. So bloody rude. I should be used to it, as it happens everywhere and it never gets any easier. I always feel that Daisy becomes the entertainment when we enter a room, and she didn't disappoint today.

With her various noises, clapping and fake coughing, she put on a show. When her name was called for the audience with a consultant, she decided to keep him waiting. She was providing a show. She threw her shoe in the direction of the staring twat man, but unfortunately it missed him – damn her aim!

With the bribe of music on my phone and a fresh dummy, Harvey and I managed to herd her into the room with a new audience. Her fabulous consultant – whom we've known for over twelve years – knew he had to be quick with his questioning.

Students passed sympathetic smiles to each other. Without much hesitation, he decided her anti-epilepsy medications needed increasing. There will be a new medication to sort the problems she seems to be having with her circulation (but I want to research it first so that's on hold for the moment) and he also wants to play with her sleeping medication. Now that's definitely worth a shot! Bring it on!

March 30th
Hippotherapy

I bet not many of you have been kicked (really bloody hard, might I add) in the stomach this morning? All I was doing was changing her bum, but I think the fact it was her third nappy of the morning was the reason for her irritation. I should just let her sit in poop all day and see how she likes it!

What started out as a relatively calm (early) morning, did escalate to me disliking Daisy very quickly. All sorts of thoughts go through your head when your own child physically hurts you; anger, hate, sadness, disappointment, but above all PAIN. She kicks like a mule!

Dressing and medicating didn't go quite so smoothly either. Far too many attempts, a couple of near miss slaps (I move very quickly when I need to) and a drink, book and iPad hurled in my direction. Ha ha, missed! I managed to appease Daisy with some Quavers before her transport picked her up for school. Her mood softened and she forgot she didn't like me anymore. However, I didn't even attempt to brush her hair, I value my life too much. I choose my battles. She'd just have to rock the 'just got out of bed' look today.

Hippotherapy to those of us not in the know, is the use of horses for physical, occupational, speech and language therapy (and not as Nick thought, is me saying Daisy was having therapy).

Daisy is very lucky to have access to it through her school. She had a session today. I didn't need to read it in her school book to know, as when she came home, she constantly pointed to a horse in a book, clapping and smiling – see she's not daft – while quacking.

Oh OK, maybe she is, plus she was covered in mud! I'm really happy though, as I believe Daisy is benefiting from this form of therapy, so it's nice she has an activity she can engage in. Even if she can't make a horse noise, a quack will do!

I'm yet to see any pictures and I'm guessing she can't sit on a horse. The poor horse would get a hernia, but the fact that she came home in a much nicer mood than when she left for school is good enough for me and if Daisy is happy, we are all happy.

March 31st
BWP - Bloody Wood Pigeon

Today was a good day. Daisy only woke twice in the night. OK, so we were downstairs just after 5.00am, but that was due to the wood pigeon again. BWP as I like to call him (bastard wood pigeon), has now reached the prestigious place of being top of my 'who I'm going to kill with a gun when they become legal after Brexit' list.

The list does worry me, as it's a very long list. Very, very long. Cardiff's gene pool will diminish if I do get my hands on a little Kalashnikov, so maybe it's best if my list just stays in my head!

Daisy was a delight for the first two hours this morning. When I say delight, what I really mean, is she was compliant with nappy change, medication, dressing, breakfast and second nappy change. After two hours she got a bit narky with me. She did hit out and hiss like a snake a few times for no reason, but nothing too troublesome. Not too keen on having her hair plaited either, so that was a bit of a rushed job while I sang my favourite 'Postman Pat, Postman Pat, Postman Pat is a big fat tw*t.'

Oh, I do love to change the words, keeps me sane! I don't think the increase in her medication last night could have worked miracles quite so quickly, so she must just be feeling nice and calm today, which is just dandy.

Off to school she trotted with no second glance for me. I do feel sad when I see her sitting in the mini bus. She has no expression, she just looks blank. I wonder what she thinks, can she think?

I had a day off today (probably along with half the NHS). We have to use our leave up (use it or lose it), so to make me feel good about myself, I watched Jeremy Kyle. Gosh the teeth on that show, the tracky bottoms!

A meeting at 2.30pm regarding respite for Daisy was hopefully a success (time will tell), so all-in-all like I said, today was a good day. Chin, chin, wine and Housewives of Cheshire are calling!

April 2nd

Move Over Shakespeare

Bedding blowing in the breeze.
Birds are chirping in the tree.
Daisy sits upon fresh bed.
Nappy off she does a wee.

Next step try to dress her.
She isn't up for it.
So stands in-front of bedroom window
And flashes both her t**s.

Now it's the turn of medicine.
This is going to be fun.
She wallops me with a *Fimbles'* toy.
Now where's that bloody gun.

Its 7.00am on Sunday.
I look like a bag of shit.
So make-up on and flick my hair.
Let's just get on with it!

D aisy has been silent today, happy(ish), but silent. Her arms are mottled again and her hands are blue, ice cold with black knuckles. I can't tell you the anxiety this causes me. It makes me so sad to think she can't tell me if she is in pain or uncomfortable. She keeps clenching her fists, which to me indicates some discomfort or pain, but who knows?

Her consultant has prescribed a new medication which will start tomorrow, so hopefully, it will help, but as with most treatments for Daisy it's a guessing game. Again, I feel so bad I am giving her another medication that may or may not help her or may give her nasty side effects, which in turn, I have no idea if she is getting them. She cannot communicate her feelings, it's such an awful predicament but one I have to try. Poor Roo, life's so unfair.

April 3rd
My Little Hulk

A gain Daisy slept quite well and I do think the different formulation of her sleeping medicine is making a difference. She didn't wake until 5.00am, and believe me, that's bearable. It's bloody typical of Daisy's impeccable timing though, as her father is due home on Thursday for two weeks. I'd planned he would spend some 'quality' time with his little girl at approximately 11.00pm, 1.00am, 2.30am and 4.00am every night! Just my luck!

When she did wake this morning she was still silent. No wiggling or jiggling to *The Tweenies,* no smiles, no claps, nothing. If anyone could see (or hear) me in the morning they would think I was crackers, as I converse with a child who couldn't care less what I say as long as I feed, dress and change her.

There was a blip when I was dressing her for school and she decided the time wasn't right. She went into *The Incredible Hulk* guise, completely ripping off her vest. Grrrarghhh – that was my response not hers. She's so, so strong! She also didn't want a hair brushing session, so out came the iPad, iPhone, Argos catalogue, Quavers and a very annoying musical *Fifi and the Flowertops'* toy. Distractions abound and taking my life in my hands, hair brushing was swift but successful. No one would notice the knots.

Medicating was semi-successful, as long as you accept I had to straddle her armed with a Jammy Dodger biscuit in my mouth, then squirt the medicine in whilst letting her take the biscuit from my mouth. Anyone who saw me in work though would have noticed telltale medication splattered over my tunic, as I didn't have time to change after it splashed back, but I'm past the point of caring about my appearance in work. I guess that's a slippery slope I'm going down. Oh dear! Work couldn't come soon enough, I needed the respite.

Home from school still silent. Still no circulation in lower arms, hands are stone cold. My little pet managed to eat a rather large chicken dinner though and loved every morsel apart from the secret medication laced spoonful of peas. Mmmm Mummy's cooking!

Bath, she loved it and actually gave me a little hum of *EastEnders* theme tune and the Jacuzzi prompted a rendition of Jingle Bells. Desperate for bed, she didn't take much rocking. I hope she has a comfortable and sweet dreamed night.

April 4th
Moody Madam

I knew from the moment she opened her eyes this morning that Daisy was in a foul mood. She stomped out of her bedroom and not only did her nappy leak onto her own bed, but due to me not being quick enough to steer her from my bed she managed to wet that as well. So by 6.00am this morning there were two lots of washing in the machine.

Once downstairs, her mood didn't lighten. She was on a mission to destroy, swiping at anything in reach including me. I served her breakfast hoping that would appease her, but she just threw my offerings across the kitchen then pointed and moaned. A really annoying moan until I picked it all up – toast, marmite side down!

Dressing was a staged process one piece at a time, each removed several times until she knew I'd eventually win. Every minute of this morning was a battle. She wanted my head on a stick and me hers.

Is it wrong to hate your child sometimes? I did today, but then I noticed her clenching her fist tight and punching her head. Realising she may be suffering, my feelings of being a crap mum surfaced again. I'm trying my best to help her, but I'm failing miserably, as I can't seem to keep her happy.

Daisy is in respite tonight. I would normally feel guilt, but just for tonight I'm going to enjoy the peace. I'd considered drinking myself into a coma, but I'm too old to cope with the morning after hangover, so it's off to bed with a glass of water, TV on silent and a book – living the dream me!

April 6th
Twitter Troll

Well, I don't really have much to write tonight. As Daisy was causing grief in respite last night (and this morning) I've only had the pleasure of her company since 3.45pm. I have to say though, she seems nice and calm and happy to be home.

I've had a couple of 'wheeees' and 'LaLa's', so she's even found her voice a little. All chores have gone to plan. She ate all her tea, enjoyed her bath, let me oil and brush/plait her hair and is now ready for her evening medication and snoozes.

I'll use tonight's post to address the lovely kind thoughtful lady who direct messaged me on Twitter, correctly telling me I don't deserve such a special child and that I will go to Hell! Crikey, Moses! Hell!

Dear Lovely Kindhearted Lady,

Please, please message me again. I will supply you with one weeks clothing, nappies, food and medication, all the toys you could wish for and one delightful little Daisy. Any funding you require can also be arranged. You can collect Daisy – actually, I'll drop her to you – at 6.00am on Monday morning (start of school holidays).

You sound amazing and I'm sooo looking forward to

meeting you. Unfortunately, I'm also pretty confident you'll
be begging me within a day (or if she's in a good mood, a day
and a half) to take her back. I do, however, still think it's an
excellent idea for you to be the mother Daisy deserves and
give it a go! So, like I say, please contact me again, I'll unblock
you!

> *Here's hoping,*
> *Annie x*

Wish me luck!

April 10th
Coffee and Sunshine

Yesterday Daisy was an angel. Compliant, happy, calm. Taking advantage of her mood and the sunshine, we armed ourselves with supplies of crisps, biscuits, her drink, spare nappy, spare leggings, wipes, iPad, iPod, a book, her Fimbles and ventured out to share her with the world. Well, Cardiff Bay to be precise and the inevitable staring eyes.

She sat like a princess in her wheelchair. Nick did the pushing (and moaning) as she is heavy to manoeuvre around crowds. He removed her dummy as soon as she was on parade. It really bothers him that she uses one, and I agree it does look ridiculous, but he doesn't manage her twenty-four seven like I do. It is her comfort and is great to dangle in her face a bit like a 'carrot in front of a donkey' if you need to get her to move.

We have become pretty immune to the stares and giggles that always accompany a walk with Roo. We do get the sympathetic head to the side looks as well, but not as many as the ignorant glares.

Many a time have I lost it with people, but nowadays, I have to accept Daisy is not a normal member of society and that however unfortunate it is, we do not fit in this normal world.

We couldn't stop at our usual Starbucks, as it was standing room only and that is not an option for us. We need military planning. Tables need to be strategically placed in a corner so Daisy can be trapped. Chairs are used as a blocking tool and distractions are offered to our princess.

We can't sit where she can grab at people – one of her favourite pastimes – and all cups must be placed on the floor. You never know when a kick to the underside of the table will ensure your cup of coffee will be dripping into your handbag so, as there was no room, we continued on our loop of the Bay and returned to the car as thirsty as when we left it.

Some years ago, again at Starbucks on a busy sunny day, I foolishly asked two young lads if I could join their table as it was the only one with a spare seat – Nick could stand, I thought! Anyhow, they nodded in an 'are you taking the piss' sort of way and I sat anyway. I needed coffee.

I was a little aware groups of youngsters were staring and assumed it was at Daisy, as it always is. Nick arrived with the coffees, Daisy was in her wheelchair. Nick placed freshly brewed coffee onto table and Daisy kicked the table. The iPhone of the rather blinged up guy became a victim, as did his gold and very white Versace (cool aren't I?) kicks.

Of course, I got the blame from Nick. Always my fault. Why did I put my coffee on the table? Why did I sit Daisy so close to the table? But where was I supposed to put her, in the high street? Why, and this is crucial, did I choose to sit next to two premier league football stars? Well, how's a girl to know?

Nick did offer to pay for the phone, but thankfully,

blinged up guy just wanted to leave and leave quickly he did, signing autographs as he left with his grubby shoes! Ah well, he earns plenty of money and coffee only stains a bit!

I learned some valuable lessons that day, the most important being I should never assume everyone is staring at Daisy, they are not. There could be a famous football player (or Hollywood megastar – story to follow when suitable) sitting in the wings.

April 12th
Is It Still Only Week One?

Is it me, or are the Easter holidays just the most horrid weeks of the year? I feel so bloody irritated by everyone and I think it's because I hate these two weeks. Daisy has been sleeping well. She appears happy, she's healthy, so why am I so unhappy?

OK, so my husband is home and drives me potty at times, but this Easter he's actually come in useful (not often I say that). I'm using him to care for Daisy when I'm in work, but then when I come home, due to my OCD, I can't bear the mess.

I should be appreciative, but no, not me. I moan and get even more irritated. He doesn't keep the house as tidy as I would; he leaves crumbs everywhere, stuff everywhere and his work is strewn over every surface. I just feel overwhelmed by mess.

I think the problem lies with the fact that I just can't think what to do with Daisy for two weeks. She can't do what other children can do; go to the cinema, go bowling, ride a bike, go to activity clubs, go swimming (unless there is no one else in pool and it's heated to the temperature of a bath), go for a nice leisurely lunch, go shopping, etc.

You get my drift? I get it other parents struggle to entertain their kids during the school holidays, but with a child like Daisy, it's compounded one hundred times, as she doesn't even have friends. Not a single friend. She doesn't know how to play, so I can't even have children around to socialise. She can't read a book, hold a pen, do a jigsaw, finger paint – she can't do anything!

I can't tell her like my mum used to say to me endlessly 'go out and play', it's just not an option, so I feel anxiety over how to get through these two weeks. It's not a time for family for us, we are alone. It's just a time of getting through each day and counting down the hours. It's bloody suffocating.

So, it's halfway through week one, still a long way to go. I'm wishing my life away and just hoping Daisy remains happy for the next week and a half. It's a long shot, I know, but maybe, just maybe, she will remain happy – at least that will be one of us.

April 16th
Honey, I Cured the Kid!

A pparently, hay fever affects twenty-five percent of the population, so it stands to reason Daisy decides to be one of the percentage!

She started suffering about five years ago. First year, just your usual itchy eyes and sneezing but jeez, by year two she really did suffer, bless her. So, Daisy being Daisy (and also being as daft as a box of frogs), didn't just rub her eyes when they itched she actually stuck her finger in her eye sockets and rubbed from the inside!

It was absolutely horrific to witness, but we all know what its like once you start rubbing an itch, you just can't stop and Daisy was no exception to that rule.

Every antihistamine was tried, but none were a match for her index finger! So two years ago, I thought I'd try local honey as I'd read it can desensitise the body to local pollen. Crazy lady, I hear you say, and believe you me, I'm the world's number one sceptic, but what harm could it do to try it?

Six pounds and fifty pence later (better be bloody worth it), I started my daily practice of giving Daisy one tablespoon of the ridiculously messy gloop onto bread every morning.

It was great, because I could even use it as a medication trap (her anti-epilepsy sprinkles couldn't escape the honey).

I'll cut to the chase, it actually worked. Really, no joke. OK, so she still had one hay fever tablet occasionally disguised in an Oreo, but yes, it actually worked. I only had to rely on the antihistamine if she went out of town. Those bees must really be homies!

Daisy started her new course this week. It will continue until roughly the end of June. So take it from me, if you have a child who thinks scratching their eye from the inside is a good idea, try local honey. If it doesn't work, stick it on your parsnips, if it does work, thank me later!

PS: don't give to babies under twelve months – not a good idea.

April 17th
Crappy Easter!

Today was supposed to be my lie-in. Nick had offered to get up with Daisy, so I was looking forward to an extra hour in bed. Daisy woke at 4.00am. That wasn't in the plan, so I said I would try and get her to go back to sleep. An hour of me screeching (and threatening death) later, Nick could take no more and took Daisy downstairs so my lie-in could begin at 5.00am – zzzzzzzzzzzzzzz.

I bolted out of bed at 6.00am. Nick was like a mad man, screaming words you wouldn't want to hear on Easter Monday! Daisy had, in his words, 'shit everywhere', but I think the problem began when he tried to change her nappy and had to deal with an up-the-back job! I took over – bathing her, cleaning, stripping bed, steaming downstairs floor, the list goes on and on and on.

At 7.00am, my 'fresh as a Daisy' little ray of sunshine (grrrr) and I went downstairs. Me desperate for a cup of tea, Daisy in need of food to top up her empty intestines. As I walked through the hallway, I smelt a waft of nastiness in the air. Surely there can't be more poop. It's not possible, but there was a definite odour.

I checked Daisy's nappy – nothing. I knew it wasn't me, so just as I was about to question Nick, I caught a glimpse of something out of the corner of my eye. A trail of brown splodges followed me. Bloody hell, I'd trodden in shit and now I had to re-trace my steps to source it.

When I ordered my leopard print stairs and landing carpet (yes, you read correctly), I thought it was such a great purchase. It looks stunning against a white wooden hallway floor and fits in with my modern contemporary home, but – and it's a big but – you can't find 'shit' on it!

Nick and I were on our hands and knees for at least half an hour up and down the stairs smoothing our hands across the carpet looking for traces of Daisy's insides. We still haven't found it, so I'm hoping my slipper scooped up an entire lump, but I'm still on the lookout and definitely won't be barefoot anytime soon.

Happy Easter!

April 19th
Wink Wink!

H usband back in Africa. Son back in Birmingham. Just
me and madam now.

Daisy doesn't like me today, she's not in the best of
moods. It's been a very long day, 4.45am was the start and
now she's drugged, so I'm hitting the remainder of a bottle
of Prosecco.

I'm unsure if it's PMT she is suffering or the effects of
glue! You see yesterday, as it was my hubby's last day with me
for a while, I thought I'd make an effort and glam up a bit.
So, out came the falsies. No, not breasts, lashes!

I added the glue in a nice straight line and waited the
twenty seconds as instructed on the package. Damn that
instruction! Daisy saw her window of opportunity as the lashes
sat on the dressing table and assuming everything is edible
down the hatch they went.

What to do? Would they stick to the insides of her throat
and act like car wash brushes as her food went down? Surely
not? I tried to prise her mouth open, but realised this was a
bad mistake, as she tried to remove my finger with her very
sharp teeth.

I looked on the package (seriously, I actually looked) to
see if it said anything about swallowing lashes. Strangely, it

didn't. This needs to be addressed by the manufacturer in my opinion. So, I googled 'swallowing eyelash glue' and its amazing how many dogs have swallowed it!

Anyhow, assuming Daisy would have the same effect as a puppy, I think she's going to live. They have not re-appeared yet, I just hope they don't get stuck at the exit point – that would be weird looking – eww!

April 22nd

Who Knows What Tomorrow Will Bring?

Dear Daisy,

Who knows what will happen in the future? Man has been to the moon, doctors seem to perform miracles on a daily basis and your father didn't 'kick-off' when I suggested we look at a new property. So maybe, just maybe, one day your brain can be fixed.

I'm writing you this in hope that day is not in the too distant future and you will be able to understand that everything I do – everything - is to make you happy.

I was brokenhearted when I dropped you to respite yesterday. I hate doing it. I feel such guilt and it didn't help that you wouldn't look at me or bow your head for me to kiss you goodbye.

Do you hate going? Do you like going? Do you wonder if I will ever be back to pick you up? Do you care? I don't know how you feel. Everything is guesswork. You were so tetchy yesterday and I tried everything to just make you comfortable and happy, but you weren't playing my game.

I sat for what seemed like a lifetime, with you holding my finger whilst watching endless episodes of Teletubbies. *I played your favourite tune in the car (on a loop). I drove to*

205

the park to take you to the swing (which you fell off). I took you to look at the cows and horses in the field down the lane, you didn't even react to them you were so moody.

We single handedly added a big hole in the ozone layer with the miles we drove, yet when we got home, you still seemed so unhappy and irritated. Are you suffering? Are you frustrated? What can I do to help you?

Unfortunately, Daisy, you've drawn a very short straw and you're stuck with me, so we have to make the best of a bad situation. You will never want for anything. I can give you all you need (thanks to your dad), but the one thing I can't give you – yet – is a useful brain. That day will come, I'm sure of it, but until then we just have to get through each day and if you're happy, we're all happy.

I love you, Daisy,

I'm just so sad for the life I've given you x

April 25th
Oh My Giddy Aunt!

C an you get bird flu from handling a dead bird – in your mouth? Just throwing that question out there. Today, had been a really good day, that is until a bird crashed into my kitchen window (annoyingly, I had just paid an extortionate twenty-five pound to have cleaned). Sadly the bird died. This is a regular occurrence (must be those sparkling clean windows!).

I think this is bird number four to have perished due to my shiny panes, anyhow, less of the showing off, I shouldn't be proud to be a bird killer! In the past, I have had husband home to pick up and dispose of birdies or I have called upon neighbours, today I needed neither.

I studied the bird for at least five minutes through the glass until I was sure it was dead (feet pointing skyward was a bit of a giveaway, but in the past I have screamed like a banshee when they have come back to life just before imminent disposal). I decided my best course of action was to ask my neighbour John to remove it from my patio when he was free, he'd love to be the hero.

Over to John's I popped. Daisy was sitting on the kitchen sofa. John wasn't in. Daisy was not on the sofa when I returned.

Daisy was pushing her red bubble car around the garden.

Nothing unusual, she loves that car, has never fitted in it but loves to circuit the garden endlessly by pushing it around and around and around. What was unusual, though, was the black mass hanging out of her mouth. Oh my giddy aunt!

I should have known not to leave the bird uncovered. A similar incident happened years ago when she actually had most of a baby bird in her mouth (that was still half-alive) this time I felt luckier. Not only was the bird dead, but it was too big to chomp on so removal was quite easy. She was a little reluctant to hand him over at first but I offered a swap for two dummy's and feeling sick, took it out of her mouth, (bloody hell it was still warm), she couldn't resist those dummy's.

I still feel shaken up. Medicinally I have had to have several glasses of wine, so excuse my grammar. Daisy has been scrubbed, the bird is in the dog poo bin over the road and I am still in shock. So, like I asked at the beginning, can you get bird flu from handling a dead bird in your mouth? Let's hope not!

April 27th
Do Be De Doo

Daisy has been sprinkled with fairy dust today! OK, so they had to use a heck of a lot of the stuff but, nevertheless, she must have been sprinkled as she's been an angel. So different than two days ago when she had horns either side of her head and was ready to go to war with anyone in her radar.

That's the trouble with Daisy, no two days are the same. Nothing is predictable, plans cannot (and do not) go to plan and it's all depending on her mood. It unnerves me that she's so happy, because I know the bubble will burst, but I am going to enjoy her for the time being.

Anyone who's ever helped care for Daisy will know that she has a naughty noise! The naughty noise, however, is a fun noise. It's only heard when she is in a good mood. So when I heard 'doo be de doo' in a high pitched tone this morning, I knew something was up.

I followed the tune and there she was butt naked standing in her brothers bedroom window, humongous boobs displayed to the waking world. She was waving her nappy – luckily clean – like a flag and barking at a man walking his dog (who nearly walked into a lamppost).

Dear God, she is absolutely bonkers and has no shame!

I waved to the man (with two fingers) and pulled down the blind, pretty sure that one day she's going to cause a nasty accident outside our house.

Isn't it heartbreaking then, that this morning while she's in this most perfect mood, I noticed two really nasty blisters on her heels. She didn't hobble or moan, she didn't complain of pain because she can't.

I just happened to see them when I was dressing her. The skin was broken and looked really angry. She must have been in pain the day before, but couldn't tell anyone.

This I find unbearably sad. Imagine not being able to say how you feel or do anything about discomfort. Daisy has always been really tough, but still must feel pain of some sort. I usually notice any mark or bruise (ask the school) immediately, so missing these blisters has upset me. Poor little thing. Plasters on, she's oblivious. Off to school she trots.

April 29th

Controversial Klaxon

It's 4.10am on Thursday morning and I'm sitting downstairs feeling a bit shit!

Daisy has woken so many times in the night. I'm unsure how many times I actually got up. She was clearly very uncomfortable and couldn't settle herself (ibuprofen and paracetamol were no comfort), so at 4.00am I gave up and brought her downstairs.

It's too early for breakfast and even CBeebies hasn't started yet, so one of her many saved programmes on the planner goes on. *In the Night Garden* seems to have put a smile on her face.

Reason for the discomfort, you guessed it, period! I shouldn't really go into my rant, as this will probably alarm many, disgust some and downright offend others, but as I'm very tired I will.

Daisy will never have a relationship. Daisy will never have sex. Daisy does not need to suffer the pain and discomfort of periods every month for the next forty years, as she will never have a baby.

Daisy wears nappies, for goodness sake, and therefore – not meaning to sound selfish – it's not pleasant or dignified dealing with the aspect of changing her. So my question is this, why can't she have a hysterectomy?

The reason, apparently, is that she does have the right to have a baby and I would be taking that right away from her! As awful as this is going to sound, let's be clear. The only way Daisy could ever get pregnant is if she was raped!

Now, I'm all for disabled people's rights and would be the first to support any law that affected those rights, but in this case, surely the law should look at individuals and not the disabled female community as a whole?

Every case should be taken on its own merit. I don't have some master plan of whipping out the wombs of every disabled woman who walks the planet, I just want to comfort Daisy. Some have said to me that allowing Daisy to have such drastic surgery is incredibly cruel; selfish on my part and unnecessary, but I wholeheartedly disagree.

I've looked fully and thoroughly into all the options and a hysterectomy would be the right choice for us. Daisy suffers from seizures, some of those seizures are linked to her periods. Seizures could kill her one day, so apart from the monthly suffering, to me this is an extra added risk, a risk that could be removed.

This is a sore subject that doctors cannot agree on and seem very uneasy discussing. What kind of mother would choose to do this to her daughter? A good mother or a bad mother? I truly believe a good mother who only wants her daughter to have the most comfortable, pain free, happy life she can give her.

I don't know if my views are shared, I guess everyone is entitled to an opinion, but all I know is that I would never ever do anything to Daisy if I didn't believe it was in her best interests. Daisy is my priority, I will do what it takes to help her at all costs.

Watch this space!

April 30th
Armless Trip to the Shop

C rap afternoon followed by a crap night and now it is precisely 4.42am. I am sitting in the kitchen, Daisy is scoffing a banquet of offerings and bedding is having that pleasant smell of urine removed in the washer. I have very strong spoon bending coffee and bloody *Dora the Explorer* is chirping away. If I ever meet her, I'll stick that backpack...

Anyhow, Daisy had a lovely day yesterday spending time in a sensory room, then visiting a park with horses and swings. So, thinking she would be nice and calm, I took the decision to nip to M&S to get some currency for a little trip while Daisy is at Ty Hafan next weekend.

Daisy doesn't 'do' shops, so this wasn't a decision I took lightly, but as I was only running in I thought she would be fine. I parked in a great disabled spot (one benefit of Roo) right outside the doors and did wonder if I should leave her in the car. However, my sensible head got the better of me after recalling locking her in a car in the same car park a few years ago and having to get the AA to break in to rescue her and so I strapped her into her wheelchair and in we trot.

We were on a mission whizzing through the pensioners (there must have been a coach trip), dawdlers and chatters. I then made a terrible error of judgement, I stupidly tried to manoeuvre the wheelchair through an aisle that was not made for 'wide' chairs. Socks one side, a display of schoolchildren in an array of school uniforms the other.

I wasn't anticipating Daisy would decide to stick her leg out at right angles at the sight of the mannequins. We came to an abrupt stop. Daisy wasn't happy that I'd nearly removed her right limb, so took her distress out on the poor schoolboy to the left of her completely removing his arm from its socket.

It dangled in his jumper and as I was trying to 'pop it back in' she grabbed a rack of socks. She had a couple of five packs in her mouth whilst the metal rack crashed to the floor. It was at this point a lovely lady from M&S rushed over.

'Are you ok?' she gasped. 'Oh my God, is she OK?' she exclaimed.

I feigned shock, pretended to check Daisy over and assured her Daisy would be fine and that the wheelchair must have clipped the shelving.

The lady apologised to *me* asking if there was anything she could do to help! I was going to suggest shoot Daisy, but just smiled and said, 'Don't worry, it's fine.'

I handed over twenty pairs of men's pants. We left. I didn't get my currency.

May 4th
Rule the World

I should be happy right now, as I'm off on a girly 'cultured' weekend to Amsterdam in the morning. Can't wait. I've packed my case, painted my nails, had a few relaxing glasses of wine, so why am I feeling crap? Why have I cried for most of the evening? It could be the fact I miss my husband and son. I do, I really do. It could be that I'm lonely. I am, but the biggest reason is that I have left Daisy at a hospice and that aches my heart.

The hospice is the most wonderful, amazing, caring and friendly respite facility I could ever dream of sending Daisy to. However, the fact remains that it's a hospice and that means it is for children who are life limited. This I struggle with.

Daisy was being treated like a princess when I left her. She was soaking up the attention and loving every moment. She didn't care when I said goodbye, didn't turn to watch me leave, didn't understand.

When I drove the half hour drive home this evening I cried a river – bloody ridiculous isn't it? I blame Gary Barlow. No, unfortunately he wasn't in the car with me at the time, but he was singing a particular song on the radio, 'Rule the World', which always starts me off. I hope no one noticed my blubbering, as I must have looked a right state behind the wheel.

I know Daisy will have a fabulous weekend, she deserves to smile and giggle and fall about in fits of laughter. Actually, that's an inappropriate term to use for Daisy as she is an epileptic, so lets just wish for lots of laughs! Me, I'll be fine in the morning – look out Amsterdam!

May 8th
Sweet Sixteen

Tomorrow, Daisy reaches a milestone in her life. It's her sixteenth birthday.

On May the 9th in 2001 I had so many dreams for my new gorgeous baby girl. Those dreams have never materialised and never will. Instead, when out shopping for a suitable present today I have been struggling, as I do every year, to come to terms with her condition.

Tomorrow, Daisy will not tear open her presents with excitement, blow out candles on her cake or laugh and giggle as friends visit to share her special day. She won't have girlfriends over for a sleepover, get the giggles after one glass of champagne or sneak kisses with a boyfriend. No, tomorrow for Daisy it's just another day, but I will do my utmost to make it special for her.

Tomorrow I will celebrate her sixteenth. I will open her presents for her and clap hands until my palms are sore. I will feed her cake and crisps and chocolate until she can eat no more. I might be feeding her for a good while on that one! I will also give her all my attention all of the time, for this is the least I can do.

Daisy has changed our lives, but we need to celebrate and thank her tomorrow. There have been so many low points in the last sixteen years, unbearably difficult and painful, but set against that have been so many unexpected highs. She's funny, unpredictable, adorable, cheeky and she has enriched our lives.

Yes, without her, our lives would have been so different. So much easier, but in truth, so much poorer. So I'm wishing Daisy the happiest of days for tomorrow - Mummy's gorgeous, special little girl.

May 11ᵗʰ
Well Done, Daisy!

I was watching Daisy on her bedroom monitor this morning. She was just sitting up in bed, dummy sucking in and out of her mouth, rattling the bed rail furiously to get attention.

I really couldn't be bothered to get up and see to her – I just lay and watched. The rattling got more and more intense until 'snap' yet another bed rail broken. Bloody hell, why didn't I just get up. After all, it was just past 5.00am! Grrrrr.

Our morning went quite well. The newly turned sixteen-year-old was delightful. Nappy change, tick. Breakfast, tick. Dressing, tick. Medication, tick (after three attempts). Another nappy change, tick.

No remotes, make-up, food, toys, iPads, iPhones were offered to me whilst I showered. Could this be the new grown up Daisy?

Off to School. Then to Work.

Daisy arrived home and was still in this gloriously happy and compliant mood. Her food was ready and waiting and feeding went without a hitch. After dinner, I settled her beside me and put on her favourite programmes. Today, I chose Clifford the Big Red Dog. She excitedly meowed, barked, quacked and hissed. She was so happy. I was happy.

Even now after all these years, it's the small mundane things that make me stumble, which jolt dark feelings buried deep in the recesses of my mind. Opening Daisy's home/school book, I came across a certificate. It was a 'Celebrate Success' Certificate. It read:

'Congratulations to Daisy for turning the pages in the book. Well Done.'

Well Bloody Done! How can I feel pride seeing such a certificate? Turning the pages in the book! It was a stark reminder that Daisy is not your average sixteen-year-old by any stretch of the imagination. As I sat watching her programmes with her, I felt myself just staring at her.

She looks much, much younger than her years, but I guess a typical sixteen-year-old girl is nowadays caked in the latest MAC make-up anyway. She has an enviable innocence, a fuzzy, goofy, infectious smile and the amazing ability to make me feel such deep love. Daisy is oblivious to her problems and that is such a blessing. She has a pampered life, so I really should not get hung up on her certificate. I should just accept it, after all, she can turn the pages of a book for goodness sake!

Behind our front door it seems weirdly normal to have this unusual girl, sometimes manic, sometimes passive, but with a strange gift of being able to bring joy. Sometimes I want to kill her, throttle her, beat her with a big stick, but these are just wine induced threats. I would never lay a finger on Daisy, for if I did, boy she wouldn't half wallop me!

May 16th
I Hate Noddy!

Noddy had it this morning – a full on punch in his stupid peach skinned, blue-eyed, silly-hat-with-bell wearing face. It was him, the wall, or Daisy – I chose the sensible option.

My morning had started really well and Daisy was happy to be dressed and nappy-changed. She ate all her breakfast, gave lots of 'do-be-de-doo's' and lots of smiles. Then it all went wrong.

I haven't noted any outbursts recently. When I say recently, I mean a few days, as Daisy has been really happy and content. However, both school and the respite home have commented on her aggressive, out-of-the-blue behaviours where she has attacked children and adults alike. No preference, everyone's a target when she has one on her.

So, dropping my guard this morning, I drew up her medication into various syringes and armed with the obligatory custard cream biscuit, confidently took aim with the first shot. Then, 'KAPOW!'

I was launched across the room as a rather impressive kick from my precious little donkey caught me unaware. It didn't half hurt. Peeling myself off the floor, I wanted to scream, but over the years I have learned that the only way to

221

win with Daisy is to sing songs to her. After being winded and feeling like crying, and with Daisy still in need of medication, I found myself singing.

'Miss Polly had a dolly who was sick, sick, sick...'

I braced myself and took aim again, this time sitting on her left arm to prevent injury to myself. Damn her right arm and damn Noddy, who was perched within her grasp. The bell on his hat caught me and believe it or not, was bloody hard when swung at the speed of light into my face.

Furiously I straddled her and with her cheeks between my thighs squirted her medication in then ran – fast. So, that's why Noddy had it this morning. Who knows, tomorrow it might be Postman Pat and I'll take pleasure from punching the annoying twat if the chance arises.

May 21ˢᵗ
Pacified With A Pacifier

Isn't is ridiculous that a sixteen year old girl has a dummy? What type of rubbish mother allows her teenage daughter to suck away ten to the dozen on a 'da'? The answer – me? Believe me, I've tried for years many different ways to rid Daisy of this ugly facial adornment.

The vinegar trick was the first attempt, as it had worked with Harvey – on his third birthday – what a treat! He loved his dummies and hid them all over the house, so the vinegar trick had to be executed as he was now a 'big boy'. So, here's what you do:

1. Overnight, you soak all visible dummies in a bowl of malt vinegar.

2. Remove delicious vinegar flavoured dummies from vinegar and place around the house.

3. Wake your angel from their sleep.

4. Explain to them a fairy has visited in the night and as they are now three years old the time has come to be a big boy (or girl). A spell has been placed on the dummies and they will no longer like to suck them.

5. Your child will laugh in your face and upon finding their first dummy ram it in their chops – then spit it out.

6. After hesitantly testing a few more, they realise a spell

has been placed and voila – success!

Worked for Harvey a treat. Didn't work for Daisy. She loved the new flavoured dummies. Couldn't get enough of them, even placing two or three at a time in her mouth. Obviously, the spell story didn't work either, as I could've been talking Russian. She didn't understand a word.

Over the years, Daisy has gone through phases of needing or not needing her dummy. Always sucked in the night, but often daytimes we could get away with hiding them and she would forget she needed one.

School used to remove it as soon as she arrived and she would not be given it until home-time. However, during the last couple of years she has become more reliant again.

School even allow it during the day as she is more comfortable with it in class. It's her comfort. It calms her. It distracts her from other idiosyncrasies; yanking her hair out, strange involuntary mouth movements, chewing her toes.

Also, when Daisy gets upset or frustrated, she punches herself in the nose, and hard. Faced with a child wanting a dummy or breaking their own nose there's an easy choice.

Her dummy sucking doesn't bother me. It makes for an easier life. This is not the way it should be, but it's the way it is. She's sixteen, of course she shouldn't need a dummy, but she likes it. It's her vice just like wine is mine, so for that reason alone I'm not going to remove that one bit of pleasure for her anytime soon.

May 25th
And I Wonder...

I didn't know how I could write about my woes regarding looking after Daisy following the horrific Manchester atrocity, but the reality is life goes on for all of us. We cannot help those who have lost their precious lives. We can cry for the pain of the people lost and left behind, but for us that are distanced from this awfulness, we have to continue living.

My life is shadowed with what now seems trivial moaning and winging, but the world doesn't stop for those of us left in this mad, sad world. We have to carry on.

Daisy has had seizures today. Awful violent scary seizures. You'd think that after all the hundreds of seizures I've witnessed, that I would be conditioned to cope, but I'm not. They never get any easier. I despise them. It's torture to watch and I feel so impossibly helpless.

The first one was 3.10am. I bolted out of bed when I heard the gulping and distinctive 'seizure' noise. Daisy had blue lips, her eyes were rolled into the back of her head, her neck was stiff and her body tight. It lasted about three minutes.

That's a long time when you're waiting for it to end. You wonder if it will end. Is this the seizure that will end Daisy's life? That sounds dramatic doesn't it, but it's how I feel every time. The darkness does leave me as soon as she breathes again, but it's there. These wretched seizures don't just endanger her life, each one erodes her brain.

I lay next to her, holding her tight. She groaned and moaned until eventually we both fell back to sleep. 5.30am another seizure. This time, her face was in the pillow, so I had to force the pillow into the mattress so I could remove her dummy and stop her from suffocating.

Two minutes later it was over. Daisy let out an awful deep groan and entered into a phase known as 'postictal' which is a recovery phase. Daisy tends to have very long periods of postictal phase, three, four, five hours. Today's will be interrupted with more seizures, of that I have no doubt. Will I be forced to use her emergency medication? I don't know. I just have to sit and wait.

With the seizures come complete bowel evacuation. It's so difficult to clean up an unconscious sixteen stone girl. Getting the nappy off is the first hurdle, cleaning is the second, fresh nappy third, removing the sheet beneath her the fourth.

There is no help. I'm not that strong, but I have to clean her up somehow, so I do and I am knackered. Today, while sitting waiting for the next seizure, I will try not to feel sorry for myself or for Daisy. Yes, it's shit. Yes, the next two or three days will be shit, but d'you know what? It's the card we've been dealt.

We live in a shit world. So I'm sitting holding Roo and listening to Will Young sing 'Evergreen' on the radio. The words could have been written for Daisy and me. They make me sigh and a tear drops. Damn you and your lyrics Mr Young!

May 29th
Bank Holiday Blues

4.00am – four bloody am!

It's bank holiday Monday. What's wrong with this child? The rest of the world is sleeping. Even the birds can't be blamed today, as they are having a lie-in.

I hate her this morning, but Daisy is so happy. Even me shouting and screaming doesn't stop her being happy, she just is. She's pulling and prodding me, trying to talk, communicate.

She want's up and I have no choice. Well I do, but what I am feeling I would like to do right now would see me end up with a life sentence! I have to get up and I'm angry. I'm angry that my husband is in some fancy hotel somewhere in the world enjoying sleep. The neighbours are asleep, in fact everyone is asleep apart from this stupid child of mine!

I feel like I'm going to explode with rage, bitterness, jealousy. I must have been rotten in my past life. Maybe I was a mass murderer? Hang Man? Torturer? All my past lives are coming back to plague me.

Today is going to be one of the longest days ever! I'm so envious reading of all the families on their day trips and get-together's. Do people intentionally try to wind me up? Are their lives that great? The answer is probably 'no' to both questions, but that doesn't make me feel any happier.

For me its just another day of caring for this girl for whom time has stood still. No day is different. She is just happy to hold the same toy Fimble (even that she can't bloody wind), look at pictures in the same bloody books, watch the same bloody TV shows. Nothing changes, nothing has for sixteen bloody years and I'm angry.

So there we have it, Bank Holiday Monday PISS OFF!

June 23rd
Same Old Shit

I haven't written for a while, no excuses. What have you missed? In a word 'nothing'. That's the thing you see. Nothing changes, it's just the same old shit week after week. Ridiculously early mornings, an annoying silent and incredibly irritating child who demands constant attention slowly draining me.

As you can guess, I'm in a rotten mood today. It was 3.46am when I gave up trying to get Daisy back to sleep. I stupidly thought I would have a better night as the temperature had dropped to twenty-six in her room and she didn't look like she was melting for the first time this week, I was wrong! She was clapping, pointing to the TV for about twenty minutes, pulling me, tugging me, pinching and clearly she had a death wish so I thought rather than having to explain to the police why I'd murdered my daughter with a large plastic Iggle Piggle, I'd better splash my face with cold water and face another day of 'living the dream'.

Daisy is sat with me on the sofa. She is surrounded by toys she can't play with and books she can't read. Rip, yes. Read, no. They are repeatedly thrust into my face. Fireflies is playing on repeat on her iPod, it's a tune that is constant, I hate it but

I don't really hear it anymore, it's just always there, in the background, tapping away at my patience, waiting for me to snap! Today she wants 'me'. Not a great day to want 'me' as I'm grouchy but as she grabs my hand to wind up her Fimbles toy, I look at her and feel such sadness that at sixteen years old, this is her life. She is stuck in Groundhog Day. She is happy, I'm sad. She gives me a grin and a wiggle.

Over the past few weeks Daisy has had good days and bad days. Seizures, unidentified illness requiring probably unnecessary antibiotics, aggressive unprovoked behaviours, hospital appointments, dental appointment (unsuccessful), me constantly saying sorry for outbursts (not mine, hers), stripping (not me, her), more bedding washed than you'd think is humanly possible, voluntary nil by mouth days, anything-that-fits-into-her-mouth-and -can-be-swallowed-days, constipated days, complete bowel evacuation days, silent days, high pitched screaming days.

It's 5.00am now. Madam is 'yum yumming', best not keep her waiting or she'll punch herself in the snout. So there we have it, as I said, nothing changes, same old shit, different day.

June 28th
Happy Days

We have had a few good days this week which is a rarity I know. Daisy had a positive experience at Touch Trust on Saturday (a sensory session that focuses on touch and positive feelings).

I was apprehensive before the session as not only did I think it would be a complete waste of money but also Daisy had proper 'kicked off' in Costa Coffee en route, targeting the only two couples quietly enjoying their drinks, so we (Harvey was my second pair of hands) were convinced she would continue with her destructive, angry mood – we were wrong.

Daisy sat in the dedicated Touch Trust room which had a hippy-ish almost Ottoman tent vibe and waited patiently. Daisy has a strange obsession with pipes in ceilings, odd I know, so immediately spotted them and happily for the first ten minutes pointed and pointed and pointed whilst we had to keep repeating 'ooh, yeah'.

The session began. Sensibly I chose to sit on the opposite side of the room to Daisy, Harvey drew the short straw and was perched next to her on a sofa. It began with an introduction and we each, in turn, had to clap each other as a welcome. There were six of us in total. Daisy, me, Harvey, the therapist, a young man and his carer. Daisy loves to clap and doesn't understand 'taking turns' so happily clapped a lot!

A bit of weirdness followed, we had to remove negativity from our bodies by almost brushing it out with our hands. Harvey had to remove Daisy's (she would need a heck of a lot of 'brushing', but he went along with it). He held his hands close to her skin and 'whooshed' all negativity away, I couldn't look at him, I'm so immature at times. Daisy sat quite happily as all her demons were exiting her body, I smirked at Harvey. Harvey was the sensible adult and ignored me.

Next was choosing a musical instrument. The young man chose some cymbals, noisy cymbals, but he was loving the clanking they made. We clapped, a lot. Daisy's turn. She doesn't understand the concept of choosing or playing an instrument. Harvey chose a shaky bell thing, he shook it for Daisy. We clapped, a lot.

Next, Elton John – not in person, now that would've been something –, a rendition of 'Crocodile Rock'. Daisy didn't get up to dance, but was smiling and jigging on the sofa. Thinking I could just sit and enjoy the show, I was then encouraged to dance to try to entice Daisy to her feet, I threw some shapes on my imaginary dance floor but Daisy remained on the sofa, clapping. Harvey's turn to smirk.

The session ended with the lights dimming and some soft music. Daisy was still clapping while the therapist seemed to be meditating. I was grinning, Daisy was now 'yum yumming', loudly! More clapping. The hour ended and both myself and Harvey felt that it was money well spent. Strange, but a success. If Daisy can remain in a room without escaping, pushing, pinching, hitting or grabbing someone for a whole hour it's a success. We will return.

On Sunday Daisy behaved herself while out with two carers for a few hours. The previous week she was returned after less than an hour because she had hit a pregnant woman who was having a nice stroll with her family. I found myself apologising for her behaviour to the carers as I always do. The lesson to be learned is to think of possible incidents before they happen then maybe they won't happen.

Sunday afternoon drive in the car. I took my usual route which has a benefit of a Starbucks drive through so it's a win-win situation as Daisy will happily moo, quack and grunt at all forms of wildlife on her car journeys and I get my triple shot caffeine hit.

Daisy is now at Ty Hafan (children's hospice) for respite for a few days. The reports so far are promising, she's being a diva so must be enjoying herself. My anxiety due to guilt has waned. My house is clean, washing is up-to-date, all Internet purchases are being delivered to the Esso garage so hubby won't see them and so here I am catching up with all the reality shit TV that I love – *Love Island, Ex on the beach, Big Brother* – while drinking plenty of wine, eating too much chocolate and basically doing very little.

I know this period of my type of heaven won't last too long, but for now I'm enjoying not having to do much. Hubby is home tomorrow so my only job before I go to bed is to bury all the empty wine bottles in the bottom of the recycling bin.

Glass is empty, time for a top up.

July 10th
Said It Before, I Hate Mondays

I 've invented a new word. It's only ever going to be relevant to a handful of people, well to be precise just me (and my husband, very, very occasionally). Drum roll please... the word is 'Roo-lag'. I think it should be defined as 'a physiological condition that affects your ability to function in a pleasant, calm and tolerable manner due to constant sleep disturbance and ridiculously early mornings'. Symptoms include irritability, excessive eating (due to being awake for twenty hours out of of twenty-four), ugly black circles around eyes, self loathing and complete child loathing. Treatment, none found as yet. Clinical trials ongoing, but a possible solution could be in the form of a bullet right between the eyes.

I shouldn't be nasty, it's not Daisy's fault, but it's so difficult to be nice when tiredness envelopes every part of me. I think this episode of sleep disturbance is due to a tooth problem. I may be wrong but Daisy has not been eating well for quite a few weeks (hasn't lost any weight though). She is booked in for an 'urgent' tooth examination under GA but that 'urgent' request was three weeks ago and as yet there is no sign of a date. Daisy isn't like any other child. She can't go to a dentist and just open her mouth for a peek at her pearly whites, no. My bloody child needs a GA for a simple procedure. This will be her third one for tooth examination, it's horrendous, but has to be done. She can't indicate pain, she can't tell me if her mouth is throbbing or her throat is hurting. I have to guess by process of elimination. It's all guess work. Sometimes I get it wrong, mostly I get it right.

She was up at 4.30 today. Breakfast has been served since 5.30. Normally it would be demolished in minutes but today it is sat there, laced with some medication. It remains untouched. Quavers will be offered soon, I'm holding out, but inevitably they will be placed on the platter in the hope her appetite may trigger. She doesn't appear unwell, she's giving me nasty glares and I've had some high pitched screaming from her, so I'm now going to attempt to dress her and medicate her. I have a feeling this isn't going to be easy this morning.

I have to go, she's just kicked her banquet on the floor. She will be lucky to make it to school... alive, arghhhhhh!

January 26th
It's Been a Long Time

I t's been a while, I know, but you really would not have wanted to read what I had to say for the last few months! It's been very difficult, emotional, tiresome. But, hey, shit happens and now we must get on with our lives.

Daisy is amazing. Don't get me wrong, she has not sprouted angel wings in the last couple of months, but what she *has* done is shown what an incredibly strong character she is. The incomprehensible pain she suffered last year is forgotten in her world. She has forgiven me, I can see it in her goofy (bad choice of phrase) smile. Every day I'm reminded as I stare at her lost looks and I feel so sad but what's the point, I can't magic her teeth back, they have gone and she didn't even have a chance to pop them under her pillow for a pound off the tooth fairy (not sure what the going rate per tooth is nowadays but if it's more than a pound per tooth, wow, it's just as well that bitch of a dentist didn't give them back to me!) Damn, I knew my bitterness would slip in.

So, what has changed? Well, Daisy has lost quite a bit of weight, but I guess if you have twenty-one teeth butchered from your mouth and don't eat for nearly a month because the pain is so intense weight loss is inevitable. Her seizure pattern has increased, oh and she looks like a little gummy old lady! Unfortunately her sleeping pattern hasn't changed and she still insists on torturing me by rattling her bed rail at 1am, 2am and 3am. In fact, I have to say that on certain nights it's actually been her lack of teeth that has saved her life for if she hadn't given me a toothless grin I swear she would now be in the great big dentist chair in the sky!

Does Daisy care about looks? Does she heck. This blissfully unaware teenager just gets on with being Daisy, but me – being the selfish individual that I am - well I'm devastated and I doubt I'll ever get over what has happened to her. Everyone tells me you can't tell until she smiles but they lie to be kind and many would argue this, but I'm not daft!

So, here we are, 2018. Another year and who knows what will be thrown at us? Who knows what will test my patience? What I do know is that whatever happens, Daisy will remain un-phased. Me, assuming my liver holds out, will do my best to care for this incredible girl who, on alternate days, I want to love and then murder. She tests every part of me but ultimately she needs me so I will fight for her, what has happened isn't over but so far as my tedious posts go it is and no more will be said... famous last words!

February 15th
She Sleeps

I was woken at 4.45am by the awful sounds of Daisy suffering a seizure. I bolted out of bed and she was face down in her pillow, blue lips, gulping for air. I dropped the bed rail, straddled her and pushed the pillow deep into the bed so that I could remove the dummy and let her get some air. It lasted about three minutes, but felt much longer. I lay next to her and fell back to sleep.

5.50am it started all over again. This time the seizure seemed much longer but probably wasn't. However, the shaking and groaning was very alarming. I held her hand and watched her.

9.05am I decide to administer emergency medication to halt this next seizure. She sleeps.

10.30am, you get the picture...

We are now on the fifth seizure and each one has increased in intensity. It's 2.35pm and Daisy hasn't woken yet. I've tried to rouse her by talking and singing (that's enough to rouse anyone!) but she doesn't want to join the world today.

I'm hopeful there will be no more, I can only give one more dose of emergency medication, so I am praying to a God I don't believe in that she will wake soon and ask for yum yum. I fear it's going to be a long day and night but I know she will recover, she always does. This time it might take a little longer but she will soon be driving me to distraction once again, of that I can be sure.

So, I'm sitting next to her on her bed, with a hot water bottle on the base of my spine (a back ache as a result of trying to change her nappy) ordering clothes I don't need and reading stories regarding epilepsy that I shouldn't be reading. Life was never meant to be like this.

And today life sucks.

February 17ᵗʰ
I Wanna Be Weak...

You can always tell I've been awake for hours when I start wittering on about inane and uninteresting things. Today is one of those days, sorry. Best stop reading now.

Yesterday wasn't good. Daisy wasn't on the same planet as the rest of us. She was locked into her silent world with little movement (apart from her bowels – many times!) Sleep was alien to her the night before so I had only managed three hours sleep in total which doesn't do my reflection much good. I looked horrific and any small child would have run screaming from me.

We started the day half a day before the rest of the planet and by 5.00am bedding was changed, washed and drying, Daisy was zoned out on the sofa just staring at nothing, but not letting go of my hand... arghhhh, and I was watching a catch up of Trauma (I have to say, three hours of my life were wasted with that, shite ending).

The day didn't really improve. Daisy just lay like a little (cough) dead thing, not eating, drinking or interacting and to make it even worse bloody Davina McCall had replaced Holly on *This Morning*. Shoot me now.

By 3.00pm I thought it best I try to bathe Daisy. I prized my hand from hers and ran her a lovely bubbly bath. It took about forty-five minutes of coaxing to get her to follow me and she was walking like she was on the moon, but we got to the bath and it was much more pleasant sitting next to her for the following hours.

Wine time, I mean, Bedtime. Whoop whoop!

I think I fell asleep at about 8.30pm, not sure, but 1.00am was the next time I definitely remember seeing the clock. Surely she will go back to sleep? In the following hour I administered a sedative (to Daisy, not me), changed her nappy, put TV on, turned it off, screamed, swore, screamed louder, swore more. In fact, I half expected the police to break down my door, surely someone heard me scream? Course they didn't, we are alone. They say sleep is for the weak, I want to be weak!

So today, let's see, she's a bit brighter looking, she's sitting rather than lying down, she's holding her iPad to her ear listening to 'Fireflies' on repeat, she's not eaten or drunk anything, but it's early so I'm hopeful. She is still silent but giving me the odd smile. Oh, and I haven't smothered her! I do wonder if her insides are dissolving though as there can't possibly be any more nappies to change, but they keep on coming.

HAPPY SATURDAY!

February 18th

Easy Like a Sunday Morning

Seizure day. Tick.
Post-ictal day. Tick.
Lucid, lethargic day. Tick.
Post-ictal psychosis day.
ARGHHHHHHHHHHH!

Today, may possibly go down in history as the worst day, EVER, and it's only 4.30am. Carers have cancelled on me so bring on the day.

Daisy woke at 1.35am. I thought I had a plan. Medication to sedate her was by the side of the bed in preparation for her awakening. Jumping on her to syringe it in, I thought I'd won. I popped her TV on (*Postman Pat* two hour DVD) and lay her down, snuggling her into her pillow. The sound was so low only a dog would hear it. Lights off, I went back to bed so that she wouldn't be distracted by me snoring, if only! Within a minute the bed rail was rattling. Within two she was attempting to climb over said bed rail. Within three THUMP, she had.

I could tell by looking at her huge pupils that something wasn't right, I've seen it many times, my heart sank. Great, what else can be thrown at me. She stripped, ripped her nightie, punched her nose that was already congealed with dried blood, threw her drink cup that I'd offered her, clapped manically all in the space of a few minutes; all this whilst laughing in a scary way.

Post-ictal psychosis shouldn't occur in children, trust Daisy to be an exception. There is little research into it and probably none regarding mentally handicapped children but, believe me, it's horrendous to deal with. I keep a bottle of haloperidol for such occasions and have administered a low dose, but so far it's not doing its job. My only fears today are that one, she really hurts herself by punching her nose so hard or two, I really hurt myself by jumping off a cliff!

Easy like Sunday Morning!

February 19th

Bloody Cappuccino

So, day five of our current nightmare. Daisy was given so much medication last night I'm amazed she woke up! 4.00am was her lie-in over with and I was relieved that I'd gone to bed before 8.00pm. It's hard to believe that I'm actually happy with her waking so early, but after three days of being up at 1.00am, 4.00am felt like half the day had gone.

Today has been mixed. She was beyond manic for the first three hours, jumping on bed, then the sofa. Not unusual, you might think, but Daisy is a ninety-eight kilogram sixteen year old! She was laughing hysterically at nothing, punching her head, throat and nose, and running, stripping, throwing anything she could get her hands on and continually ripping any nappy I dared to put on her. This did cause me a big problem as she took the opportunity to poop on her clean bedding and then run around upstairs, I'll spare the details.

Bath.

After the bath she calmed for a bit until there was a knock on the door. A guy came to do a report on our kitchen, long story. Out came her horns and I have to say I did chuckle to myself when she 'charged' full pelt at this poor six foot two, twenty stone man, and he looked terrified! He was a great source of interest for Daisy and I'm sure he made up all the measurements as he was gone in a flash. Flash... yes she did!

As I'm slowly going mad with my own company I thought I'd take her for a drive, go for a walk and get a Starbucks. Mistake. Queuing at the drive through she suddenly took a turn for the worse. She went bluey grey, started trembling and then continuously punched her nose incredibly hard, it was like a bloodbath. I was trying to clean her nose and calm her shaking just as my cappuccino appeared through the window. I reached over with blood on my hands, apologizing I asked for a serviette and just grinned at the poor guy, who knows what he thought, probably took my registration and has reported me as we speak.

I abandoned all hopes of wheeling her round the barrage and drove home.

She has now settled again and thanks to good old McDonalds has eaten for the first time in five days, which means I can also give her ibuprofen for what must be a very sore snout.

I have no idea how long this phase will last, it will probably end just in time for her dads return on Saturday!

February 23rd

Next Choice of Sedative, A Hammer...

It's now day nine of what feels like a prison sentence. The last few days have been horrendous. Each day Daisy has not been able to settle day or night! Waking for good at 1.00am, wandering up and down the stairs, unable to sit still, constantly punching her head, throat and nose unimaginably hard and relentlessly pointing to blank walls whilst groaning and whining. This has been without doubt one of the worst periods of postictal activity EVER, and we have been through many.

Yesterday afternoon I went to collect my hubby from the airport, he was coming home. Yippee, help at last and someone sane (ish) to talk to. I thought the drive would calm Daisy so in the back of the car she was strapped (I chose the back as I didn't want her to distract me with her continual punching) and off we went on our relatively short journey. OMG, five minutes into the trip, just as I joined the motorway she chose her moment to strip. All I can say is thank goodness I have tinted rear windows. Daisy in her confused state managed to get trapped in her own dress, all I could see in the rear view mirror was her head and body hidden in a polka dot dress, arms in the air.

She was getting very, very agitated, and she wasn't the only one. I was stretching backwards while trying to steer in a straight line, to try to help her un-trap herself, but I couldn't quite reach. Then all of a sudden **RRRRIIIIIPPPPP**, off came the dress, now resembling a rag. She had built up quite a sweat and was quiet for the next leg of the journey, but not before she had removed her vest with relative ease and had decided her shoe would be best placed to join me in the front striking the windscreen en route. We arrived, in one piece, and whilst waiting for my knight in shining armour (said in jest) to appear I just took a moment to sit and look at Daisy in the mirror, naked, envious boobies on display, pointing to the headrest and mooing, how is this happening to me, us?

I was hopeful, having spoken to her consultant in the afternoon, that by increasing a hypnotic drug (chloral hydrate) to a dose that would knock a horse out, that we would enjoy a silent night. No wakings, no bed rail rattling, just silence.

Giving the drug posed it's own problems. Prescribers never consider this – how do I give large amounts just before bed, along with other drugs and try to dilute it to lessen the awful side effects? In short, it is nearly impossible, but impossible isn't a word I use so off to battle armed with four twenty millilitre syringes I went. I won.

Daisy woke five times between 7.00pm and 12.00am then 1.15am, yep, she was awake for yet another day of torture.

Daisy 1, medication 0.

May 9th

Saved Your Dad a Fortune Today!

Daisy is seventeen today. Seventeen.

No car, no handbags, no shoes, no make-up. Presents have no meaning, she's just content with me murdering the 'Happy Birthday' tune over and over and over again since 4.25am!

She's full of gummy smiles, but oblivious to the fact it's her special day. She will be showered with my attention and I will do my best not to be irritated if she won't let me change her nappy, brush her hair, dress her, feed her (hang on, that's not going to happen, her mouth has been in 'feed me' pose for a good hour!) Daisy will actually get to eat chocolate this morning as I will willingly open the chocolate buttons she always hands me in the morning, (usually they get put behind my back, out of sight, and then she's forgotten about them), but this morning I will open them. You see, that is all she needs to make her smile.

Today, for this incredible pain in the backside, it is just another Groundhog Day and for me, as with every year, it's that sad stark reminder of the girl she should have grown into. The girl I should have shared so much with, but it didn't happen. She's stuck, un-fixable.

I'm going to try to be more up-beat today, stop beating myself up. I can't change her, I can't make her something she can never be. I will celebrate the years of joy she has given us (nose growing), I will also break a weekday habit and raise a few glasses of fizz later in her honour (nose now incredibly long).

So, happy birthday, Roo, you will most definitely be the death of me but you really are my world. And not just mine, you've cast your spell on the three of us and we will love you forever.

Mummy, Daddy and Harv xxx

June 4th

Talking shit again...

When I was growing up I swear dog poo was hard and white! Yep, you read correctly. Has she finally lost the plot, I hear you say, well let me explain.

Today, I took Daisy for a lovely walk in the sunshine. When I say walk, I walked but the lazy little madam refused so she was pushed in her wheelchair. We moo'd, quacked and barked at various animals (not necessarily the correct sound matching the correct animal, well you would be stretched to find a cow in Cardiff Bay). Daisy was quite content relaxing and taking in the fresh air until she decided all that sitting down and being pushed around was thirsty work!

Gwar, Gwar, GGWWAARRRRR! She just kept repeating her word for drink over and over again. I didn't have many options, go back and pick up her cup from the car or go and buy a 'baby' cup from the closest supermarket, I chose the latter as it was the quicker choice. I picked up the pace and must have looked like one of those super fit parents that runs with a jogging buggy, however, I am neither fit, was jogging or am a super parent. I just wanted to shut her up.

Nearing the supermarket, Daisy was getting more and more frustrated by her life threatening thirst and started swiping and grabbing anyone who came close. I had to get her a drink soon Daisy DOES NOT DO WAITING!

So, we get to the shop. The choice of cups isn't great but I just buy the best of a bad lot and then buy some flavored water. I decide on using the self serve but as I reach for my purse I notice that Daisy has a piece of green plastic in her mouth. What on earth? Grappling with her at the till it soon becomes obvious that this is no ordinary green plastic bag, this little gift is a dog poo filled plastic bag!

Jesus, Where? What? How? Who? I then looked on her lap and perched between the fingers of her other hand was a small black bag, neatly tied, presumably with similar contents, however, I could not see into the black bag but my god the dog (I assume) who had once owned the contents didn't have the same diet as dogs from my day! This bag was like a bag of slime, in fact both bags were in my opinion not how I remember dog poo as a child.

Silently screaming, I fought with Daisy to retrieve both bags of shite praying that the contents wouldn't escape; swapping the bags for a dummy and my phone I was now the proud owner of two little parcels of crap. Great. What to do with them whilst paying? Is it wrong that I put them in the bin by the tills? It is, I know it is and I apologise for this selfish human act, but what's a girl to do?

Feeling unclean, we rush back to the apartment. I thought it best to disinfect Daisy before we get in the car to head home, Why didn't I just go home! Using any cleaning product I could find, she was scrubbed. Her hands will probably fall off today, but at least they are clean. We head to the car.

Lift arrives, doors open, six people greet us, Daisy stands

there with her new audience and quicker than lightening whips off her dress on the day I don't put a vest on her. The awkward look on the two guys faces was priceless. So there was Daisy, top half naked in a lift, me trying to put her dress on, her flesh touching all. Get me off the planet, please. Longest twenty seconds of my life and their lives!

And so today I have a few apologies. Sorry to the old couple by the till to the right of me, they should never have had to hear those choice words that spat out of my mouth on a sunny Sunday.

Sorry to the family of six in the lift. Yes, it was awkward. Yes, it's not something you expect when the lift opens, but hey, it was only a pair of boobs, granted big, but boobs non the less!

Sorry to myself. I said I wouldn't drink this weekend. Yet again, I let myself down. Hey ho, needs must.

December 24th
The Spirit of Christmas...

C hristmas Eve is here and my little angel is blissfully unaware of what all the fuss is about. Daisy doesn't know its Christmas tomorrow, nor does she care! It's just another day in her groundhog world. Another day of us winding her bloody Fimbles toy until our fingers are sore. Another day of enduring those fecking animals parading through a field on *Teletubbies*. Another day of feeding, changing, feeding, changing. Another day of just hoping our little cherub will remain in a good mood. Just another day. But hey, where's my Christmas spirit. Gin, my friend, you will be poured copiously as soon as I finish work.

This year I've decided to not let all those 'making memories' tales on social media piss me off as they regularly do. No, instead I'll smile (through gritted teeth) at other's perfect festivities. I have my own reason to smile and that's down to something as simple as Daisy being happy (please, if there is a God, let it continue) and that's all it takes. Mind you, if Santa fancies indulging me with a Rolex this year, who am I to stop the big man!

So, I'm putting a positive spin on this whole Christmas charade as I believe I'm the lucky one so I want to gloat. You see I don't have the agonising pressures most parents have of getting my teenager the latest 'fad', the latest iPhone, the latest designer wear. Oh no, my little princess wants for nothing, and nothing is pretty much what she's getting this year. So, what's the latest must-have in our seventeen year old's stocking, I hear you say? Drum roll, please... a replacement copy (there's only one page left in the original) of *My First 100 Animal Pictures.* Actually, I'll have you know, it took intensive Internet searching to find!

Daisy will be absolutely delighted (I guess?), she will point and moo and meow and quack to her little hearts content, and then once I've had enough of saying 'oh yes, a cow' for the hundredth time, I will hide the bloody book, glug some gin and chuck her a copy of a shredded Argos catalogue to peruse. Simple pleasures. Deep sigh.

So yes, Christmas will come and go just like any other day in our household. The lights are twinkling outside, the candles are flickering inside and the world will think we are celebrating, but all we are doing is going through the motions. Tomorrow, the next day and the days after remain on repeat, however, just for the festive period (OK I lie) I may indulge in an extra tipple to make it seem that little less mundane.

Chin chin, everyone. x